How to Pass A LEVELS and GNVQs

THIRD EDITION

Howard Barlow

KOGAN
PAGE

To Mary, Araminta, Leander and Douglas

'Read not to contradict or confute,
Nor to believe and take for granted,
But to weigh and consider.'

'To extend awareness of your own
Needs, expectations, feelings,
From which will flow your own
Conclusions, goals, actions.'

'It is for you to decide.'

First published in 1985
Second edition 1988
Entitled *How to Succeed in A Levels*
Third edition 1995

Kogan Page Limited
120 Pentonville Road
London N1 9JN

British Library Cataloguing in Publication Data

A CIP record for this book is available from the British Library.

ISBN 0 7494 1556 8

Typeset by Saxon Graphics Ltd, Derby
Printed and bound in Great Britain by Clays Ltd, St Ives plc

Contents

Preface to the Third Edition

Since the second edition seven years ago, there have been occasional updates on points of detail, but for this third edition, the book has been created anew.

While the book is exam-centred on A Levels and GNVQs, rather than a general book on study skills, this edition nevertheless gives a very wide and comprehensive coverage of studying and related matters. I have continued to aim for clear and concise entries, with a text offering plenty of places to start and stop, so that one can identify information easily, and dip in and out. I hope the tone stimulates and gives a 'lift'. There is more on the ever more important psychological side. The book is created both out of research and out of close contact with students; I have included only what I sense is of real, practical use.

Principally, this book takes into account what one can only call the GNVQ revolution. GNVQs were set up as a small offshoot of NVQ work, and no-one anticipated the extent to which they would take off. They are still new, and will develop further, but they have secured a firm place in the educational scene. The information on GNVQs could not simply be bolted on to an existing text on A Levels.

I have tried in Chapter 1 to make clear the now more complex range and mix of qualifications, and Chapter 2 on Starting your Courses covers not only GNVQs but also has more on the theoretical foundation of successful study.

Chapter 3 on Finding Information covers recent developments in information technology, and I am grateful to the library staff of the University of Sussex, and of Lewes Tertiary College, for their useful input. Chapter 4 on Note-Making now includes note-making on computer, and I thank my local neighbourhood engineers at SSP Pumps and Johnson Pumps for their kind help which will be apparent in one of the examples.

Chapter 5 on Essay Writing has been completely re-written, and I am grateful to John Kiteley of the University of Oxford for his comments on an early draft. The essay on Richard II is reproduced by kind permission of Wolsey Hall, Oxford.

Chapter 6 covers Other Essentials, and has new material on delivering a talk and on business English. Chapter 7 on Time and A Levels now covers modular A Levels, as well as the traditional format.

Chapter 8 on Time and GNVQs is wholly new, Chapter 9 on A Level Coursework has only minor changes, but Chapter 10 on the GNVQ Portfolio is also new.

Chapter 11 on the Psychology of Study is now followed by a new Chapter 12 on the Techniques of Mental Management. I am conscious of contributions from Professor Andrew Steptoe and Dr George Hamber, but I am principally in debt to Dr David Mason Brown, a former GP now practising as a psychotherapist, whose deep humanity and stimulating insight provided much of the material.

Chapter 13 on Revision now includes some GNVQ material, and a section on key points to make revision more effective. Chapter 14 on A Level Examinations has only slight changes, but Chapter 15 on the GNVQ Tests is new.

Chapter 16 on Aiming for the Future has been considerably re-written to include course choice by computer, recent experience with the UCAS form and with university interviews, and the whole task of finding employment in recessionary times. I recognise the dynamic spark of Dr Jacky Tivers (University of Surrey) in what I have written about the UCAS form.

I thank my Kogan Page Editor for her unwavering friendliness, expertise and professionalism which have been an immeasurable asset. I am as ever grateful to Donald Markwell, Fellow of Merton College, Oxford, for his continued interest and kindness and to my family for their good-natured endurance during the trance-like states of the creative process.

How to Use This Book

The following additional tables may help you to get the best out of this book:

An Advanced GNVQ course

Chapter 1

Choosing Your Courses After GCSE

This book aims to give concise, practical advice. It is comprehensive, and covers choosing your courses, succeeding in them and moving on to higher education or employment. All the skills are included, as well as the mental aspects. The book is broken down into small units, so that you can identify information easily, and dip in and out of the text. The text is geared to achieving the highest grades in A Level, and Distinction in the Advanced GNVQ.

1.1 A Levels

A Levels are for students whose interests lie in academic study. They are the main entry qualifications for university.

The traditional rule of thumb is: you need four GCSEs at grade C to do two A Levels and you need five (or six) GCSEs at grade C (or B) to do three A Levels.

You can calculate your likely A Level results based on your GCSE results: allow 7 points for a GCSE grade A, 6 for a B and so on; add up your grade scores in English, Maths and the best five other subjects; multiply your total GCSE score by 1.05 and subtract 29.46; convert the score into A Level grades allowing 10 points for a grade A, 8 for a grade B and so on down to 2 for an E pass. If you did excellently at GCSE, the formula will underestimate your likely A Level grades, eg if you got seven As at GCSE, you are likely to get BBB at A Level, or better; it is more dependable for lower scores.

You probably need 32 points from your GCSEs to take A Levels successfully (for example, four Cs and three Ds would give you

32 points on the above GCSE points scale). If you start A Levels with between 32 and 36 GCSE points, monitor your progress carefully in the first few weeks of your A Level courses.

These calculations are only very rough guides, by no means infallible: some colleges are good at teaching students with low GCSEs, and your motivation is very important.

1. Are A Levels for you?

Yes if:

(a) you like concepts, theories and principles
(b) depth study interests you
(c) you like studying on your own
(d) you like analytical thinking
(e) you like quite a bit of direct teaching
(f) you like an emphasis on traditional exams
(g) you don't like coursework
(h) you want to keep university and career options as open as possible
(i) you may want courses such as medicine, dentistry or veterinary science, or a career in the professions
(j) you may apply to a top employer who will look at your A Level grades as well as at your degree class (eg, Kleinwort Benson)
(k) you like subjects which are not life-relevant, though some are (eg, business studies, politics and sociology).

2. Choose your A Levels on the basis of what you are good at, in a good combination.

A Level Maths is a very important subject. Apart from being important in its own right, it comes into and helps Physics and Chemistry. As an example, all universities offering Chemistry degrees like A Level Maths. If you wish to take a Maths degree, two Maths subjects at A Level are a help, but if you take only one Maths subject, it must be Pure.

A Level Chemistry is a very important science. It is the science you can least afford to drop. It is also the most representative of the sciences, being both descriptive and analytic (Biology is descriptive; Physics is analytic). It helps Biology A Level.

Thus we get only two ideal science combinations at A Level.

Maths, Chemistry and Physics
The Maths helps both the Chemistry and the Physics. This is the best combination of any A Levels. Very few science-orientated careers are excluded.

Maths, Chemistry and Biology
The Maths helps the Chemistry, and the Chemistry helps the Biology. This is the other ideal combination, although rather more careers are normally excluded with this combination than with the previous combination, eg engineering.

Another two science combinations are often studied

Biology, Physics and Chemistry
This is possible, but you haven't the Maths to help the Physics and Chemistry, and you cut out careers dependent on Maths such as engineering, physics and statistics.

Biology with two arts A Levels
Science degrees are closed, but if you have a supporting science at GCSE, you can aim for paramedical careers like physiotherapy, though this will not be easy. However, Biology is harder without Chemistry, and Chemistry needs Maths, so this is not an ideal combination.

Finally, one can look at other combinations of A Levels, ie arts A Levels

Science careers are shut, but many others are open, eg accountancy, hotel and catering.

Hold on to Maths, and take it as an A Level if you can, combining it with arts subjects. It doesn't need sciences with it: it stands alone, and you will find it of value. It goes well with Business Studies and Geography (or with Physics and Geography, if your Physics will stand it).

Be cautious about subjects with a practical element such as Art, Music and Home Economics. They are valuable subjects but are sometimes regarded askance. Look at other subjects first. Unless there is a special reason to the contrary, these are safest seen as third choice subjects if you are short. The same goes for General Studies A Level.

Try to choose a good combination, eg History, Geography and Business Studies; or History, English and a modern language. History, English and Geography are often done as a trio, but the load of reading is heavy. There is much to be said for choosing compatible subjects.

3. Now give cautious consideration to AS Levels

The traditional curriculum of three A Levels is more specialised than almost anywhere in the world. AS Levels are to encourage its broadening, as 75 per cent of people now at school will change their *type* of job three times in their lifetime. There is also a growing trend towards mixing A Levels, so bridging the arts–science divide.

AS Levels are Advanced Supplementary Levels. They are half the workload and study time of an A Level, but for that half are intellectually as demanding. Some are based on A Levels with the content reduced; others are new. AS Levels can complement A Levels if they are in the same broad subject area. They can also contrast with A Levels if they are in a different subject area, so A Level scientists can keep a foreign language, and A Level arts students can keep Maths, for instance.

For their general entry requirement to degree courses, no university insists on three A Levels as a minimum. Universities require two A Levels as a minimum, but are happy to accept two AS Levels as equal to a third A Level. Some universities will accept one A Level plus two AS Levels as a minimum, and some will accept four AS Levels as a minimum. As a course requirement, universities often mention specific A Levels which you must have.

Two factors have hindered the introduction of AS Levels. First, some schools do not offer them. Second, many students do not like the idea of achieving, say, a B grade in each of two AS Levels, in order to equate with a B grade in one A Level.

A number of possible permutations of A Levels and AS Levels have arisen, the most common of which are:

(a) *Three A Levels.* This is the traditional package: and there is safety in tradition. You will not be disadvantaged in any way by omitting to choose AS Levels.

(b) *Three A Levels plus one AS Level.* You have the solidity of the traditional package coupled with the width of an AS Level, especially if it is in a contrasting subject. In a way, the best of both worlds! The AS Level could be in a complementary subject as an alternative: you could thus continue with Maths, Physics, Chemistry and Biology.

(c) *Two A Levels plus two AS Levels.* The universities are happy with this combination, and like the idea of the gradual introduction of AS Levels. But remember you will have to do well in four subjects instead of in three; and bear in mind that certain A Levels may be specified as course requirements for some courses.

(d) *Two A Levels plus one AS Level.* A good idea for the less strong candidate, but older universities are likely to look for the other AS Level in practice, especially where there is competition for places. However, this combination is perfectly acceptable for entering new universities and for entering other careers post-A Level.

1.2 GNVQs

GNVQs are General National Vocational Qualifications. They were introduced in the early 1990s and are aimed primarily at 16–19 year old students in full-time study. Each relates to a broad vocational area but will also develop your general education. They are academically demanding but with vocational relevance. Though not a job qualification, a GNVQ can help you get a job, or you can go on with your education. There are GNVQs in the following subjects:

- Art
- Business
- Construction
- Distribution
- Engineering
- Health and Social Care
- Hospitality and Catering
- Information Technology
- Land-Based Industries
- Leisure and Tourism
- Management
- Manufacturing
- Media

- Performing Arts
- Science

You take one GNVQ, though you can also do other studies as well.
  GNVQs are at the following *levels*:

- Foundation (1 year)
- Intermediate (1 year)
- Advanced (2 years)

Management is at Advanced only. You need no previous qualifications to start a Foundation (equivalent to four GCSEs, D–G); you need one or two GCSEs A–D or a Foundation, to start an Intermediate (equivalent to four GCSEs A–C); and you need four GCSEs A–C or an Intermediate to start an Advanced GNVQ (equivalent to two A Levels, or three if six additional units are taken).

The *structure* of all GNVQs is similar. You have to take mandatory units plus some optional units. You also have to reach a minimum standard in the core skills units Communication, IT and Number. On top of this, additional units can be selected from any GNVQ at the same level, and extra core skills units can be taken in Improving Own Learning, and in Working with Others.

You are *assessed* mainly by coursework, with some external tests. You automatically pass if your portfolio of coursework meets all the criteria of the mandatory, optional and core skills units and you have also been successful in the external tests (which are on the mandatory units). Your assessors are your teachers, but there are also internal and external verifiers. A pass in an advanced GNVQ equals two A Levels at D or E grade, but you can also get a merit (equal to two A Levels at grade C) or a distinction (equal to two A Levels at grade A or B).

1. Are GNVQs for you?

Yes if:

(a) you like the practical application of knowledge
(b) you want a life-relevant course
(c) you want to improve your employment prospects
(d) you like coursework
(e) working as a team appeals to you
(f) you like problem-solving

(g) you may want higher education in an area related to your GNVQ

(h) you don't like too much formal teaching

(i) A Levels do not appeal, given that a significant minority of students either drop out or do not achieve a pass in any one subject

(j) you want a middle pathway between academic A Levels and occupational NVQs.

(k) you don't like traditional written exams

(l) you like a very specific syllabus.

2. Are GNVQs acceptable to universities?

Broadly speaking, yes: by both the newer and the older universities. But there are some cautions to add. GNVQs are relatively new and took off faster than expected, so there were inevitable teething problems. Awareness of GNVQs varies. They are not as yet a familiar university entry qualification, but universities know they are here to stay, recognise them, and are informing themselves about them.

Though the Advanced GNVQ is equivalent to two A Levels, you need some form of additional study, such as one A Level (good because they are known qualifications), or six additional units at Advanced GNVQ.

Bear in mind:

(a) You must comply if a degree course requirement wants a particular level of attainment in a named A Level.

(b) A research-based A Level (eg, Sociology, Economics) is better than a skills-based one (eg, Accounts) because it involves conceptual and analytical thinking.

(c) An A Level in a contrasting subject is likely to strengthen your hand, as you get breadth.

(d) Go for additional Advanced GNVQ units, and not an A Level, if that is right for you.

(e) Additional Advanced GNVQ units should be in a different area.

(f) If your GNVQ relates to your university course, your application is stronger.

(g) The new universities (former polytechnics), rather than the older universities, have more courses in areas similar to GNVQs.

(h) GNVQs are not the ideal preparation for any degree course in which the emphasis is academic. GNVQs are of little relevance to very traditional degrees.

(i) GNVQs are not suitable for degrees which require a large amount of background technical knowledge (eg, Maths or Modern Languages).

(j) Predicted high grades at Advanced GNVQ and A Level in your reference help a lot.

(k) Explain your portfolio carefully in interview.

(l) If you have a good range of GCSE 'passes' (including English and Maths), your choice of an Advanced GNVQ will not be seen as a forced one.

The publication 'GNVQs and Higher Education: entry requirements' gives very detailed data on how acceptable GNVQs are for specific courses at specific universities. It is available from NCVQ, 222 Euston Road, London NW1 2BZ. Especially check Advanced GNVQs in Health and Social Care and in Science.

You are strongly advised to consult admissions tutors for your course at the very earliest possible stage, to avoid misunderstanding or possible disappointment later on.

1.3 NVQs

A word on NVQs, to see how they differ from GNVQs. An NVQ indicates that you are competent to do a job at a certain level (there are five Levels). NVQs are available for most jobs. They are suitable if you have decided on your job.

1. *Where can you take them?* You can do NVQs while you are in full-time work. Some employers provide NVQ training, or local providers come in, or you attend part-time at a local college of further education. NVQs can also be taken full-time at local colleges.

2. *What is the main emphasis?* It's on showing that you can perform tasks in the workplace, or under conditions that are as similar as possible. An assessor looks for evidence that you can consistently carry out a job to the required standard. There are no externally set tests. You pass or you don't; you are competent or you aren't; there is no credit or distinction.

1.4 Extra GCSEs

Remember you need a grade C or above if your GCSE is to count in the eyes of universities and professional bodies. You need to consider at least the following:

- *English*: vital.
- *Maths*: important for most jobs and courses. Some universities require Maths GCSE (or a science subject at GCSE) for all entrants. If you have no Maths GCSE, you restrict your degree choice in Geography, Agriculture, Social Science, Psychology, Environmental Science and Biology, for instance.
- *A foreign language*: lack of one at GCSE would restrict degree course choice in English and History. Cambridge (and Oxford, in spirit) require a foreign language for entry to any of their degree courses.
- *Science*: if you are interested in science as a career, it was traditionally wise to study Physics, Chemistry and Biology as separate subjects to GCSE. Many schools now run only the GCSE Double Award in Science, which would suffice. Beauty therapy, physiotherapy and home economics courses, as examples, look for science success at GCSE.

1.5 Mixing courses

If you wish you can combine A Levels, AS Levels, GNVQs, NVQs and GCSEs. Your studies will invariably have one main focus, though. Here are some possible combinations:

- Advanced GNVQ and one A Level
- Advanced GNVQ and two AS Levels
- Advanced GNVQ and one AS Level
- Foundation GNVQ and two GCSEs
- Intermediate GNVQ and one GCSE
- Advanced GNVQ and one or two units of an NVQ
- Two A Levels and some Advanced GNVQ units.

1.6 Checking your choices

It is very wise indeed to protect yourself by checking your course choices against future university or career requirements. You will also find more flexibility than you imagined (eg, in requirements for medicine; also, it is possible to do a Biology degree without Chemistry A Level, and an Engineering degree without Physics A Level). You can write direct to the institutions you are considering (which is best). Also there are some useful books which you should consult.

1. Checking university requirements

University and College Entrance: the Official Guide obtainable from Sheed and Ward, 14 Coopers Row, London EC3N 2BH (a bit heavy going, but thorough)

Compendium of Higher Education, two volumes, obtainable from Laser Advisory Council, 21 Bedford Square, London WC1B 3HH (clear layout, easy to use, recommended)

GNVQs and Higher Education, obtainable from NCVQ, 222 Euston Road, London NW1 2BZ (easy-to-find details of how each course at each university reacts to GNVQs; a 'must').

2. Checking careers requirements

Occupations, obtainable from COIC, PO Box 348, Bristol BS99 7FE (detailed, authoritative but heavy)

The Careers Guide, obtainable from Cascaid, County Hall, Glenfield, Leicester LE3 8YZ (shorter, very helpful, clear)

Routes to a Career, obtainable from Econotext, 10 Ward Grove, Myton Grange, Warwick CV34 6QL (one side per career, tells you just what you want to know).

Chapter 2
Starting Your Courses Successfully

It is very good for your morale to begin a course successfully. You then view yourself positively, your teachers view you positively too, and further success is generated.

2.1 Starting A Levels

Success, and enjoyment in depth, come from really cherishing your subjects, or really 'getting into them'. This involves personal commitment, and going beyond the standard requirements. For example:

1. *English Literature.* Success requires your own *personal* engagement with, and response to, the texts. Hence knowledge of the texts is paramount. *Beyond* the set texts, there are other books by the authors to be read, and books by other writers in those genres, as well as theatre visits.
2. *Modern Languages.* A visit to the country where the language is spoken is an enormous help. This can be arranged through an exchange scheme with a school or a family. Such visits not only increase your standard of oral ability, they also develop an active and intelligent interest in the country's life and institutions, thus generating the use of more abstract and evaluative language (the distinguishing mark of an A Level candidate). Seeing foreign films and listening to relevant broadcasts widen your knowledge of the country and language.
3. *Geography.* Fieldwork is an essential element. Journals are an essential supplement to formal reading in order to keep up to date, for Geography is a developing subject. For example,

to study Western Europe it is necessary to be aware of EU policies and their implementation.

4. *Art*. A good knowledge of the history of art is most helpful, whether or not there is a specific paper on it in your A Level. Visits to galleries, museums and exhibitions widen and deepen awareness even if no notes are taken.

5. *Sciences*. Practical work becomes more important, and gives scope for personal observation and individual initiative. A Biology dissection involves drawing what you actually see (aided by a hand-held lens), rather than drawing what you think you should see. In a Physics practical, a preliminary investigation of the range of values possible is helpful in determining the intervals at which readings are to be taken. After the graph has been plotted, a further check of readings or additional values may well be essential to determine more precisely the shape of the line. Chemistry experiments involve careful and precise observation on your part. You infer a conclusion from your observations and test your inference by performing an experiment of your own devising. The onus is on you. Do read scientific journals. Arguably, the processes of modern science can barely be understood without a sense of the tradition of experiment and making research public.

2.2 Starting GNVQs

There are some things that will excite you about GNVQs. There are also some things to watch when you start. Pay very careful attention in your induction programme.

1. Things that will excite you

(a) The courses are very much a partnership between teachers and students. This excites your teachers, too.
(b) You feel responsible for your own achievements; you are truly independent.
(c) The focus on the real and the relevant will motivate and stimulate you.

2. Things to watch out for

(a) You must develop intimate familiarity with the *unit specifica-*

tions (or syllabus). You must work directly with them, so that you know what evidence to collect for your portfolio. One piece of work can satisfy parts of a number of different units. You have to be familiar with the unit specifications so that you can take advantage of opportunities that arise. Be like a detective: hunt out evidence for your portfolio. For example, working on a vocational unit can provide evidence on a number of core skills.

(b) Realise that there is *emphasis* on individual and group projects, role play, oral presentations, case studies and work experience.

(c) Make sure you get plenty of *work experience* placement time. Real experience is essential in order to develop a real grasp of your vocational area: professionals can give you insight. Also, you will be able to cite this practical experience to potential employers.

(d) Get to grips with the *documentation* right from the start. Some of it you may feel is excessive and confusing. You must keep your work organised, indexed and cross-referenced.

(e) Make sure you know about *'accreditation of prior learning'* (or APL). For example, some of what you did in GCSE for IT, Maths and English can probably count towards your GNVQ. But it must match the details of the unit specifications. Your GNVQ is concerned with the use of IT, Number and Communication, not the study of these. If you are not told about APL, ask. Also consult the useful book by Susan Simosko entitled *Get Qualifications for What you Know and Can Do: A Personal Guide to APL* (Kogan Page, 1992).

(f) It is essential to get *feedback* on your work right from the start. Feedback is one of the most important factors in efficient learning. Do not be unsure how you are getting on; if you don't get feedback, ask. In the extra core skill unit Improving Own Learning, seeking and using feedback is stressed. Remember feedback can come not just from your teachers, but also from other students, supervisors and so on.

2.3 Group discussion

Group discussion is vital at A Level because it refines your ideas to a higher level, helping you to achieve a higher grade. Group discussion is also important in GNVQs because it is a common means of dealing with problems in the business and commercial environment. Discussion is specifically cited in the core skill Communication.

In being a member of a group, you face a *conflict*. On the one hand, you can withdraw from the group into silence; you are then safe, but you feel isolated. On the other hand, you can become involved in the group by speaking; this is fine when people agree with you and you then feel elated, but when they disagree, are hostile or think you foolish, you can feel persecuted and rejected.

The solution is to develop a realistic but *positive attitude* towards groups. The key is to have a genuine interest in, and respect for, the views of others. From this, all else follows: the group accepts you; you feel accepted and talk; the group responds. In the last analysis, it is not a matter of being outgoing or confident. In forming your attitude towards groups, remember:

1. prepare in advance
2. be friendly
3. expect agreement and disagreement, but see them both as leading to creativity and progress
4. organise and write up jottings taken during the discussion

Next, be sure to help the group *develop*. This is a sensitive and important task. You should:

1. Be receptive. Listen attentively. Interest shown, even if silently, is a positive contribution. Make sure you can see everyone, as you need to take in not just what people say, but also their facial expressions and gestures. Circular or rectangular seating arrangements are best.
2. Ask people to clarify what they mean if you are unclear.
3. Raise a question to which you do not know the answer. Lack of knowledge is an opportunity to learn, not a problem to hide.
4. Summarise what has been said when you feel the discussion needs pulling together.
5. Help with group silence. Silence can be productive, when material is being digested. But if it is unproductive, and extends beyond its natural limit, try to put into words what you think the problem is. Perhaps the topic is too hard, or unmentionable, or there is temporary friction between group

members. Talking about the problem promotes its resolution. Encourage others to contribute.

Finally, make a *contribution*:

1. Isolate a key idea mentioned and elaborate on it.
2. Suggest a new line.
3. Give your opinions, and the evidence that goes with them, though without taking all the limelight. Your manner and tone must be right. By giving your opinions to the group, you will find that they come back improved and developed.
4. Remember the technique of 're-expressing points': re-express your own points differently if you sense that the others don't understand them; re-express other people's points in your own words to check your own understanding.

2.4 Group phenomena

When groups are being created, they go through four *stages*:

1. Forming, where roles emerge.
2. Storming, a period of instability when roles are modified.
3. Norming, when behavioural patterns are established.
4. Performing, when cohesion emerges.

You will then notice *group phenomena* operating, such as:

1. *Dependency*. This is where everyone expects the teacher to provide all the answers. Students seem to feel they know nothing and have nothing to contribute.
2. *Pairing*. Two members of the group can pair up in dialogue. Everyone else listens on the sidelines.
3. *'Fighting'*. A kind of 'fighting' can occur in groups as when an attack is made on, say, the syllabus or an alleged inadequacy in the public library.
4. *'Flight'* from the subject matter can occur, for instance by absence, lateness, senseless objections, idle chat or 'switching off'.

In an extreme form, these phenomena hinder the work of the group, and it is rare for them to be entirely absent.

The *cure* is to stick to the task of the group, then these phenomena will be harnessed to it. In general terms, the task is to find greater understanding of a topic through co-operative effort. The teacher, though in control, will tend to allocate him- or herself equal status with the students in order to aid this co-operation. More specifically, each session will have its own special task. It is important not to divert from the task on the vast majority of occasions, and allow only for the occasional digression which, though irrelevant at the time, is truly productive in a wider sense.

2.5 Working on your own

The GCSE examination is designed for all students. A Levels and Advanced GNVQs are for those students who choose to stay in education beyond the school leaving age, to be followed in a good many cases by university. Hence they feel different from GCSEs. The diagram opposite explains why.

A Levels and GNVQs are dependent to a much greater extent on students studying and learning independently. Work assignments are much more open-ended. A subject called French, say, in year 11 is not the same as a subject called French in year 12. The teacher's expectations will be different. You have to pick up new cues.

As advanced work requires a personal understanding and appreciation in depth, it is understandable that private study is very important. You are your own taskmaster, under your own control, making your own decisions. You choose how and when to study, setting your own balance between work and leisure. It is essential to work steadily throughout your course. There is a lot to do: A Level students, and even more so GNVQ students, can underestimate the load.

2.6 Thinking

A key aim in advanced study to develop as a pleasant person who thinks. The prime requirement is *intellectual curiosity*. This leads to intellectual conviction, which you then justify from evidence.

Being well read is a powerful stimulus to intellectual curiosity. Read widely, not only within your subjects but also outside them. Acquire a knowledge of current affairs: the 'leaders' in *The Times*, *Telegraph*, *Independent* and *Guardian* are useful. Try to include in

Why A Levels and GNVQs feel different from GCSEs

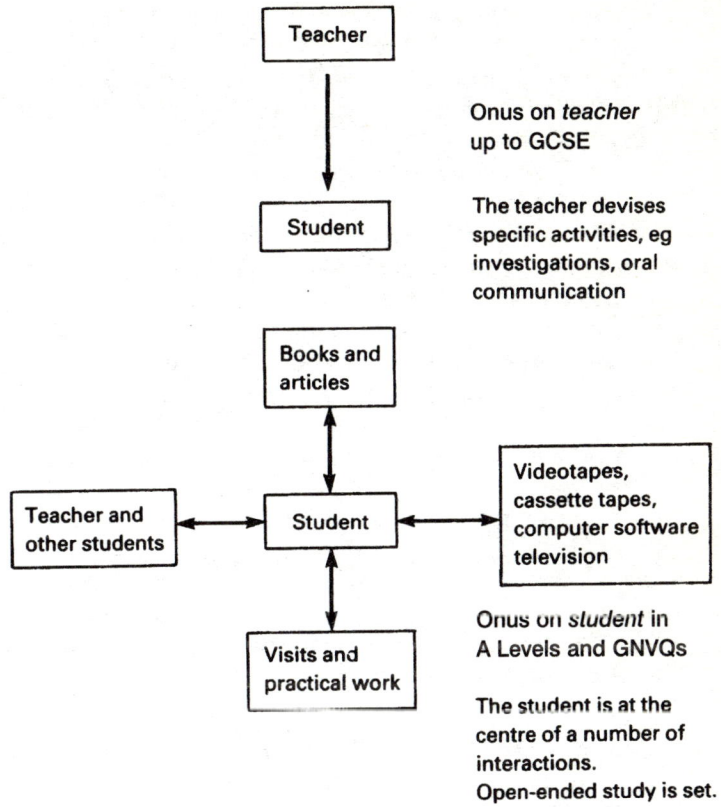

Onus on *teacher* up to GCSE

The teacher devises specific activities, eg investigations, oral communication

Onus on *student* in A Levels and GNVQs

The student is at the centre of a number of interactions. Open-ended study is set.

your thinking morality, law, art, music and literature. Keep a cuttings book and an index: A Level syllabuses are becoming increasingly topical, and GNVQs have always been life-relevant.

Share your thoughts, advance a definite line and think on your feet. When a new idea is raised, adjust your mental jigsaw to cope with it. You might first ask a question. You could then cite evidence against the idea, adopt it, or take the middle course and modify your view. Suppose someone says Eliot is a lousy poet. Avoid simply sitting and looking horrified; think and respond.

GCSE has helped you to think, so some of the techniques will be familiar; others will be new.

1. *Fact and opinion.* An important distinction to bear in mind. With facts, the evidence *amounts to* certainty; with opinions, the evidence *falls short of* certainty. In judging expert opinion, ask yourself if the authority is an expert in that field, using up-to-date knowledge in an objective way. Even expert opinion may be biased.

2. *Bias* should be identified before an argument is judged. It can arise from the choice of emotive words: 'rebellion' has a negative bias, 'uprising' a positive one. Bias can also arise from generalisations. These may be valid (if there is enough evidence), invalid (if there is insufficient evidence), or valid if qualified. A newspaper headline may state that dole claimants do not want to find work, but if the figures cited in the article amount to only a small percentage of dole claimants, the qualification *some* is needed. The GNVQ core skill Communication asks you to consider the 'reasons for bias', ie types of bias. These are: unsubstantiated information, misleading presentation of information and omission of relevant information.

3. *Empathy.* It is important to be able to give coherent expression to different viewpoints. Empathy means putting yourself in someone else's shoes (while remaining separate from them) in order to understand how things seem from their point of view. Proceed thus:

   (a) Express how they *feel*. A vocabulary of feeling words is essential. You can make a table, using the one below as a start. Use your own opinion. Be alert to the precise shade of meaning each word has. This is usually clear from the word's root, so use a detailed dictionary.

   (b) Understand their *situation*.

   (c) Link their *feeling* with their *situation*. For example, a woman in a factory may feel oppressed. Her situation is a machine environment. Thus one could say: 'She feels oppressed because she is working in a machine environment.'

   Empathy means understanding, not judging, which is a separate process where you bestow values. Nor is it the same as sympathy, which implies feeling pity and wanting to help. Sympathy and empathy may or may not go together.

Table of some feeling words useful for empathy work

	Words describing feeling good	Words describing feeling bad
Strong	exultant	distraught
	elated	aggrieved
	jubilant	depressed
	joyous	oppressed
Medium	happy	despondent
	glad	deflated
	cheerful	downhearted
	optimistic	apprehensive
Weak	pleased	troubled
	fortunate	miserable
	contented	bemused

4. *Conceptual thinking.* Distinguish between the following questions:

   (a) 'Is Britain a member of the EC?' is a question of *fact.*
   (b) 'Should Britain belong to the EC?' is a question of *judgement.*
   (c) 'Do you feel yourself to be a European?' is a question of *concept.*

You must first set out the criteria which make up a European-feeling person. Go for the crucial criteria, the points that really matter. In deciding on the criteria, think of clear-cut cases falling both within, and outside, the concept; don't forget to include the negative angle, a most useful angle in all thinking. You may sometimes need to provide two analyses of a concept, one which includes the case in question, and one which does not. Questions can be both of judgement and of concept (eg, 'Should you feel yourself to be a European?'). The classic work on conceptual thinking is: Wilson, J (1963) *Thinking with Concepts*, Cambridge: CUP.

   Individual GNVQs and A Levels have their own special concepts for detailed analysis (eg, the concept of irony in English Literature).

5. *Moral thinking.* Issues of right and wrong often arise in discussion. It is useful to bear in mind some moral systems. The

Rights Theorist might cite the United Nations Declaration of Human Rights, while the Biblical Fundamentalist will refer to the literal words of the Bible. The Cultural Relativist holds that there are no right or wrong answers to moral problems: cultures develop their own standards and cannot be compared. The Utilitarian believes an action is right which produces the greatest good for the greatest number; while an Agent-Centred Theorist might look at the motivation of the doer, and argue that an action is right if it is right-motivated. A Situationist may argue that each situation must be treated separately, and that the right action must be felt out. It is an interesting exercise to think through the implications of each standpoint.

6. *Problem-solving*. This is very much a part of the GCSE examination. You will have done a good deal of it; for example, investigations in Mathematics. The steps behind all problem-solving are worth bearing in mind:

    (a) *Objective*: What am I trying to achieve?
    (b) *Givens*: What am I told?
    (c) *Operations*: How can I manipulate what I'm told?
    (d) *Conclusion*: What is my result?

Problems are best solved step by step.

7. *Decision making*. This is a specialised form of problem-solving which you will use, for example, when you decide what to do after A Levels. Again, a step-by-step policy is effective:

    (a) *Problem*: What exactly is the problem?
    (b) *Alternatives*: What is my evaluation of the alternatives?
    (c) *Priority*: What are the priorities which the decision must meet?
    (d) *Choice*: Which alternative do I choose?
    (e) *Action*: What action must I now take?

Problem-solving and decision-making are very important in GNVQs, more so than in A Levels.

2.7 Two keys to successful study

There are two keys to all successful study for examinations.

1. You must '*deep process*' knowledge. You do this by:

    (a) interacting critically with the content of your course

(b) relating new knowledge to previous knowledge and to everyday life

(c) focusing on evidence, logic, conclusions and relationships

(d) grasping the key concepts

(e) reorganising new information into a personally meaningful framework, so that you could explain it to someone else.

The opposite is 'surface processing', which is essentially unreflective learning. Material is recorded without proper selection, and there is over-reliance on memorisation.

2. You must also work *'strategically'*. You do this by:

(a) good organisation

(b) effective time management

(c) cue-seeking (ie, finding out what gets marks, and what is likely to come up)

(d) being aggressively motivated to succeed.

A non-strategic approach usually involves too much social life and a too relaxed attitude towards deadlines.

2.8 Your own learning style

You can improve your performance by working out the ways in which you learn best. In other words, by being conscious of your learning style. Try to use as many different methods of acquiring knowledge as you feel comfortable with. Here are some terms put in pairs for convenience, but each does not rule out the other:

1. Do you prefer words or numbers? The words person studies best by reading, writing and discussing; the numbers person by problem-solving and experimenting.

2. Are you more visual or auditory? Do you see your notes as you learn them, and do you like diagrams, or do you prefer to read your notes aloud?

3. Do you prefer to use your hands and body, rather than study theory? If so, you should focus on things such as role play, manipulating equipment, field trips, and writing.

4. Are you more social or intuitive, ie do you prefer group discussion or one-to-one discussion with a colleague or tutor?

5. Do you like to see the overall picture first, then fit in the details; or do you prefer to start with the details, then build

up the overall picture? Most people have a preference. Some subjects demand one approach, some the other. Generally, it is best to go: whole, parts, then back to whole.

6. Are you a 'lark' or an 'owl', ie do you work best early in the day or later?

7. Are you musically inclined or not? If you are, you may be able to use it to help you study.

The brain produces delta waves when you are deeply asleep; theta waves when you are between waking and sleeping; alpha waves when you are relaxed but alert; and beta waves when you are wide awake and going about life normally.

The alpha state is best for studying. It can be brought on by listening to Baroque music such as that of Corelli, Bach, Vivaldi or Handel before you begin. Try Vivaldi's *Four Seasons* or Handel's *Water Music*.

Chapter 3

Finding Information

You will find one theme running through this chapter: the importance of structure. All knowledge is stored and presented in a structured way, and the effective acquiring of knowledge depends on recognising that structure.

Structure is important in other fields too. Andrew Lloyd Webber, the composer of the music for *Jesus Christ Superstar* and *The Phantom of the Opera*, made the point that ' . . . structure is the most important thing in a musical. Of course, the content has to be good too, but you can have the most marvellous song in the wrong place in a show, and it can be a complete disaster. Equally, you can have some indifferent material that comes across very well because the show is so cleverly constructed.'

3.1 Search skills

A library can be a daunting place. You can feel quite at sea there. You will feel better when you have identified some typical land-marks. In the case of a large college library, these are:

1. *The entrance and exit gates*, part of a library's security system. They protect all items in the library.
2. *The enquiry desk*. Books are issued by, and returned to, staff at this desk.
3. *Newspapers*. A number of weeklies and dailies are available. Back copies are stored for three months. There may be a cuttings file, arranged by subject. *The Times* may be available on compact disc (CD), which you get from the enquiry desk and read on the library compact disc computer (CD-ROM, or compact disc–read only memory).
4. *Periodicals*. Current copies are displayed, back copies are

shelved in boxes, arranged in each case alphabetically by title.

5. *Reference books*. These can be used only in the library, and include: atlases, dictionaries, encyclopedias, examination syllabuses (with past papers), standard textbooks, statistical data and university prospectuses.

6. *Videos, audio cassettes and CDs*. These may be available, for use on the library equipment.

7. *Books for loan*. Fiction and non-fiction, available on long or short loan.

8. *The computer catalogue*. This lists all the library's books. You can search by author, title or subject. Most libraries use the Dewey Decimal Classification System, so when you find the book on the computer, it will have a number and then letters, eg 338 ARM. The number denotes the subject. Books are shelved first by number, and then alphabetically by the letters, which are the first three letters of the author's surname. In the above example, the book is: Armstrong, M (1993) *A Handbook of Management Techniques*, London: Kogan Page. The computer will tell you if the book is in the library, out on loan, on order or missing.

3.2 Types of reading

Once you have found your material, you have to decide what to do next. You might think that you just read it, as you would a novel for enjoyment. However, do not be afraid to reject parts of books, or even whole books, if they do not meet your needs, or if you don't like them. You have more choice than you think: few books are so important that, even if you don't like them, you have to read them, and not substitutes which you like better.

To work most efficiently, you have to ask yourself one key question: *Why am I reading this*?

1. *For the general gist of a topic – use BROWSING*. This means looking through a book in a leisurely way. It is useful when you're just beginning to get to grips with a new area, because it helps you to formulate better search questions. It is also useful for wide reading. To browse, you open the book, explore, and read parts here and there.

2. *For a specific piece of information – use SCANNING*. Look up the

item in the index and write down all the page numbers on a slip of paper (this is much quicker than looking up the item several times in the index). Then scan over the relevant pages to find the information you want.

3. *For the main points and significant details – use SKIMMING.* Skimming is selective reading: you look over the chapter and select certain bits to read. In particular, you read the first sentences of each paragraph. They contain much information, and tell you where to focus your attention. You also look at: the introduction of the chapter, its headings, tables, pictures, diagrams and conclusion. But you will tend to do this automatically if you read the first sentences of each paragraph. Skimming is a useful, respectable yet much neglected practice in studying; but we all do it every day, when reading newspapers. An alternative technique for skim reading is: run your eyes down the centre of the page. Many people find this highly effective.

4. *For mastery – use INTENSIVE READING.* Skim first, then read closely, looking for three things: indicators (eg, first, second, third), conclusions and reasons. If you own the book, you can use a soft pencil in the following way (rubbing the marks out later):

   (a) indicators – put circles round them   ◯
   (b) conclusions – underline them   _____
   (c) reasons – put pointed brackets round them <   >

3.3 Quicker reading and better understanding

There has been much study and research into the improvement of reading, but as yet not total agreement on how this can be done. However, one way of describing what happens when a good reader reads is in terms of the conducted coach tour. The coach drives smoothly past the sights of interest at quite a fast speed, though it slows down when there is something of importance to see. The traveller does not attend equally to everything he passes; he takes in especially the main sights, on which the guide gives a commentary.

There are a number of important points that arise from this metaphor:

1. Move your eyes *smoothly* across the lines. Actually, they move

in little jumps, but don't think of it like that. Think of moving them smoothly across the lines. In this way you hold the drift of the argument in the forefront of your mind, and cut out looking back over the last few words (called regression). Read groups of words: these contain the thought units. Let punctuation help you.

2. Move your eyes across the lines *as quickly as you can*, but their speed of movement must vary according to the nature of the text. A difficult text must be taken more slowly.

3. Hear your *inner voice speaking the key words*. Many words on a page are very common ones, such as 'the' and 'a'. We see them so often that we understand them by sight alone. It is the less familiar words which need to be heard. Hearing can be confined to a very limited proportion of words, but this is achieved by only the fastest readers. With inner speech, your lips and vocal chords do not actually move: that would be subvocalisation. Subvocalisation tends to limit your reading rate to that of speaking, and should be avoided.

4. *Don't get too close to the book*. If reading is a type of sightseeing, you fail to appreciate the view if you are too close. Keep the book away from you so that you can take in the groups of words more easily. If you are not using a pile of books as a book rest, and are holding the book tilted backwards, the bend in your arm should be about 120 degrees. Distance also cuts out side-to-side head movements, which are tiring.

These points will need practising. Here is a formula which summarises what to do to improve your reading technique:

HOLD THE BOOK AT BENT ARM'S LENGTH.

MOVE YOUR EYES SMOOTHLY ACROSS THE LINES AS FAST AS THE TEXT WILL ALLOW.

HEAR YOUR INNER VOICE SPEAK THE KEY WORDS.

3.4 Examples of reading skills

Here are two examples of these techniques in action:

1. *Advanced GNVQ in Business*
    You are investigating the four institutions of the European Community, as part of the unit on Business and the European Community.

    - You look at the DTI publication 'The Single Market: the Facts'. On looking at the index and table of contents, it seems irrelevant. But on flicking through the introduction, you find some quite brief details, plus a useful picture.
    - You look at a book by Goodman. The table of contents says it will be relevant, with two pages covering each institution. Looks even briefer than the DTI publication.
    - The HMSO booklet called 'European Union' has some details, but it looks less immediately clear.
    - A book by Geddes has a chapter on the four institutions, but it is detailed.

    Conclusion: an intensive read for the relevant bits of Goodman and the DTI publication, then a skim read for the other two.

2. *English Literature A Level*
    When writing an essay, the use of a short, simple chapter to find your bearings, coupled with points skimmed from a good range of sources, can produce an effective result. Unquestionably the key skill to practise is skimming. It is important not only in its own right for 'gutting' a chapter, but also as the first step in intensive reading: quick skimming gives you a good general idea of the text as a skeleton on which to base a closer and complete reading. It is the hallmark of a good reader. To illuminate the value of skimming, the first sentences of paragraphs from an article on *Coriolanus* are shown on p 38. Read them carefully.

    If you were using skimming to extract the main points on the political angle of the play, you would realise you need to read the second paragraph only; if you were using skimming as the first step in intensive reading to gain a complete mastery of the article, then you would have an excellent idea of the content before detailed reading.

Skimming: from an article on *Coriolanus*, showing only the first sentences of paragraphs (not to scale).

Coriolanus was probably first performed in 1608. _____
_____
_____

Although *Coriolanus* is deeply concerned with politics, it remains uncertain what Shakespeare's own position was, if any. _____
_____
_____
_____

Coriolanus is certainly a play that provokes interference: the hero is markedly less sympathetic than Shakespeare's tragic heroes usually are, and it has often been felt that something must be done to make up for this supposed inadequacy. _____
_____

It is true that the audience does not often feel close to *Coriolanus*; not many people on the stage do either. _____
_____
_____

The person who finally stops *Coriolanus* in his revengeful tracks is the person who first set him on his destructive course, his mother. _____
_____
_____

The combination of forces which finally defeats Coriolanus is formidable. _____
_____
_____

Most of Shakespeare's tragic heroes have too much human feeling for their own good; Coriolanus seems to have too little. _____
_____
_____
_____

Chapter 4

Making Notes

The next concern is the importance of structure in the setting out and recording of knowledge, that is to say, the importance of structure in notes.

4.1 Making notes

Notes are made, rather than taken. Note-making is a creative process. It involves *judging* the relevance of material to your objective, *rejecting* what is not relevant, *selecting* the important points and *fusing* the chosen material into a new structure.

It is unfortunate that the word 'note' carries the connotation 'scrappy'. A good note is exactly the opposite: it is organised, or structured, with great care, and the structure must be readily apparent. In this way the mind can grasp the note. Note-making is the imposition of your own structure on to chosen material. A note is not a facsimile of the textbook; it is a selective 'visual picture' of a topic from which, because of its structure, the main aspects 'spring out at you'.

Before making a note, it is essential to have your objective very clear in your mind. Otherwise you do not know what to reject; everything seems important. There is a theory of management in industry called MBO (management by objective) which believes that you get things done by having clear objectives or targets.

One way of reading a chapter intensively and making notes on it is:

1. *Skim.* Acquire a general idea of the chapter by giving it a quick skim.
2. *Read.* Ideally, do not make notes at first, simply read for understanding. It is hard to make a good selection of material at this

stage. Things noted now may seem unnecessary in retrospect. However, if you own the book, with a soft pencil, make light vertical marks in the margin opposite the points to which you will return. Now you don't feel you are missing anything. You do, of course, erase the marks at the end. Light pencil marks are suggested, and if made as described and later erased, less damage is done to books than turning down the corners of the pages. If you don't own the book, write down page number and topic.

3. *Scan*. Look back over the chapter to select information which is important to your objective. You now have the material in perspective and can select skilfully.

4. *Make notes*. This comes last. Note-making is a recall activity. Tear up sheets of A4 paper into quarters. Write only on one side of each piece. Start a new piece of paper for each major point. When you have finished reading all the material, the pieces of paper can be grouped into small piles, each pile dealing with one aspect of the title. These piles become sub-headings in the note.

   It is no use making notes from one book, then from another, and tacking the second set of points beneath the first on the same sheet of A4 paper. Material from different sources has to be integrated into one note. This takes time, but it is time well spent. While you are moving material around, you are thinking and learning. (For a fast lecture, write on one side of each sheet of paper and afterwards cut up the sheets into strips, then group them.)

The finished product could look like the blueprint opposite.

Following it there is a note made for A Level Economic and Social History. A number of books have been used, because you will see that different authors are cited; but a new whole has been created from these parts. The note is certainly a visual picture, and the key aspects spring out at you.

A blueprint for the structure of a note

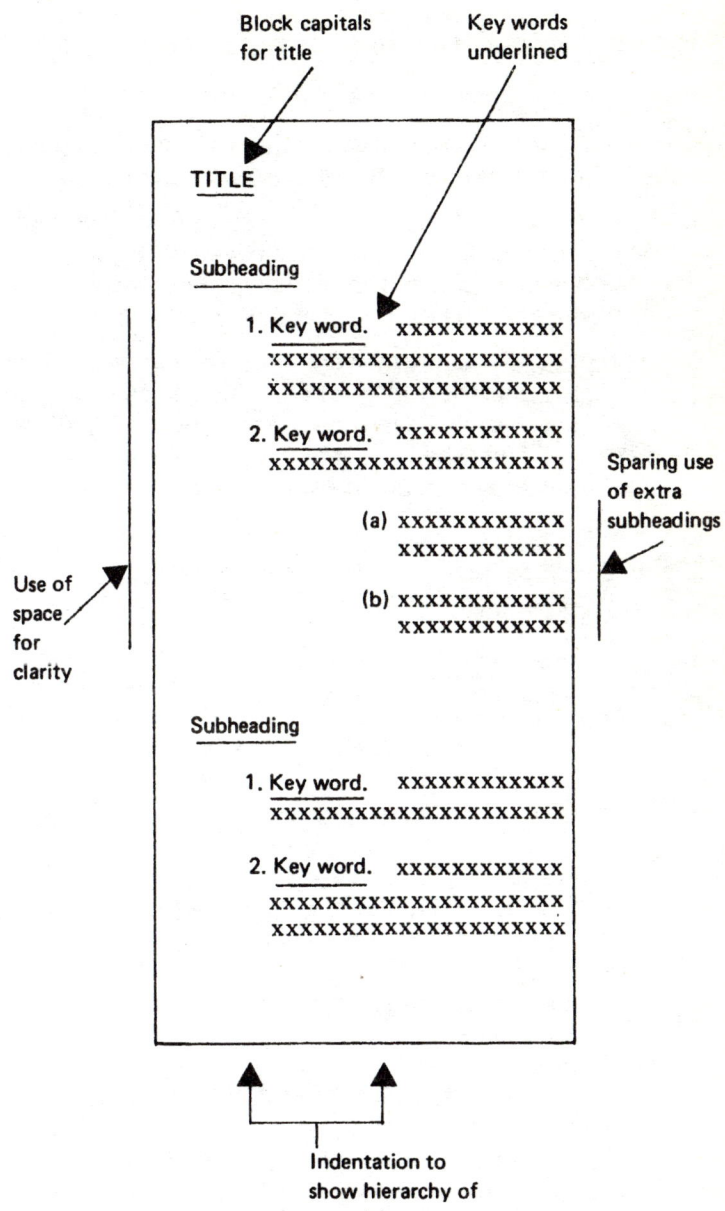

An example of a note for A level Economic History

THE MOTOR VEHICLE INDUSTRY BETWEEN THE WARS

Pre-war: many small firms, hand production

Before the war, the car industry was very like industry generally before the Industrial Revolution, ie cottage industry.

1. Small firms. There were 200 or so small firms, some of which went bust. The ones that survived did a good job. Their heads tended to be skilled engineers who wanted to produce perfect machines and price was no object.

2. High prices. Thus prices were high. The car was a rich man's toy until the 1930s, when it became an ordinary man's possession. Sayers says that a town of 16,000 in 1914 would have had about four cars. The most important pre-war by-product of cars was the bus service in London.

Post-war: a few large firms, mass production

A four-point process.

1. There was a big demand for cars. The car was much less limited than the train. Real wages were rising, thus more people could afford cars. The demand was protected because of the MacKenna Duties, which covered cars.

2. Mass production was necesssary to satisfy this demand.
    (a) Mass production involves buying components instead of making them, then the car is assembled as it moves across the shop floor.
    (b) Mass production involved concentrating on popular demand, because it was expensive to make a new model.
    (c) Mass production was emerging pre-war in America (Ford) and in England (Morris). Wartime mass production of shells proved its value. By 1930, car manufacture was a major industry but there were still a lot of design changes and it was fairly crude. Full-blooded mass production comes in the late 1930s.

Cont...

3. <u>Mass production requires larger firms.</u> Between the wars, larger firms were emerging. They did this by expansion (Morris) or by takeover (Rootes bought up Hillman). Pollard says that 'in this period, the number of car-makers fell from 96 in 1922 to 20 in 1939'. Of the 20, six of them turned out 90 per cent of British cars.

4. <u>Mass production meant lower prices.</u> A private car costing £500 in 1922 cost £325 in 1926. Falling prices stimulated demand. Aldcroft and Dyos state that 'rapid fall in prices and the improvement in the technical performance of motor vehicles together with the rise in real incomes were undoubtedly the main factors contributing to the growth of motor transport in the inter-war years'.

Below is a note on the manufacturing process, relevant to the Advanced GNVQ in Manufacturing, made after a visit to an engineering firm to acquire general familiarisation of how a small firm works. The 12 stages in the manufacturing process are clearly shown. Extra sub-headings are used sparingly (only once).

An example of a note for Advanced GNVQ Manufacturing

THE MANUFACTURING PROCESS IN A SMALL FIRM

1. <u>Customer need</u>
Some firms design 'specials' to meet the specific requirements of a customer. Discussion with the customer to find out exactly what he is trying to achieve.

2. <u>Engineering design</u>
The designers talk to the manufacturing and sales people. A solution is proposed to the customer.

3. <u>Customer's order</u>
The customer's order states what he wishes to purchase and when he would like it delivered. He receives an acknowledgement:

Cont...

    (a) the acknowledgement is the contract between the firm and the customer, to supply an item, at a price, on a date;

    (b) the acknowledgement is entered into the computerised business system.

4. Engineering detailing

Attention is given to the parts required. These may be standard parts, or ones not made before. These parts are also entered into the computer system.

5. Material control

A sophisticated computer technique is used to make sure that the parts are made or bought at the right time. A firm cannot afford to stock all the different parts, so there must be a balance between what you have and what you will need in the future.

6. Purchasing

The purchasing dept places orders with suppliers who can meet the delivery and quality requirements at the best price.

7. Production control

This dept organises the resources to make the parts at the right time, of the right quality, at the right cost.

8. Manufacturing

The production foremen organise the people who work the machines, so that both are used effectively.

9. Assembly and test

The item is assembled by a fitter, who then tests the unit.

10. Inspection and despatch

The item is checked to see that it meets the customer's requirements. Arrangements are then made for it to be packed and sent by road, rail or air, as appropriate.

11. Invoicing

The customer is invoiced and the order is closed, but the invoice is outstanding until the money has been received.

12. After-sales service and spares

The customer is kept in touch with, to make sure that the item gives continued performance. Spares are stocked and there is a rebuild service for units requiring extensive repairs.

For Maths notes, it is particularly important to include verbal explanation. This is often overlooked. The ideal structure of a Maths note is:

Instruction (to perform an operation)	Working out (with equals signs aligned)	Explanation (or comment)
Integrate between the limits O and Q	$W = \int_{O}^{Q} V\,dQ$	
	$W = \int_{O}^{Q} \dfrac{Q}{C}\,dQ$	where C is a constant
	$= \frac{1}{2}\, Q^2/C$	

For vocabulary notes, it is better to go beyond just word and meaning, and adopt the following structure:

Word	Sentence	Meaning	Association (for memory)
emploi	Beaucoup de mes amis vont quitter l'école en juillet pour trouver un emploi.	job	employment

4.2 Alternatives to notes

There are alternatives to traditional notes. Your personal preference and the nature of your task may from time to time encourage you to use them.

Annotated diagrams

Annotated diagrams can be used, for example, to produce a sketch map in Geography, and a drawing in Biology.

(a) Make a clear diagram of the *structure*, keeping it simple, without excessive detail. This is vital.
(b) Add annotations. An annotation is a written comment at the end of a specific labelling line. It talks about the *function* of the structure indicated.

Annotated diagrams relate structure to function. For example, an annotated sketch map could bring out the relationship between the physical geography of an area and its communications. They save long prose accounts, and have visual appeal. Rate them highly. Remember to include a title. In an exam, do not repeat in prose what your annotated diagram has already conveyed. The map opposite is the kind of thing to accompany a map work answer at A Level. Usually, an annotated diagram would be simpler, like the one of Ullapool below, which was quickly produced and which scored high marks in an examination. Sketch maps could be used in GNVQ Business, to show the location of shops, for instance.

Annotated sketch map of Ullapool

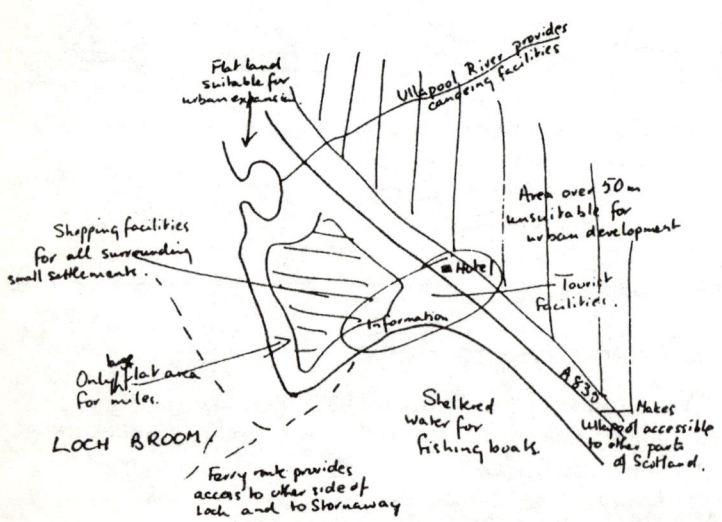

Annotated sketch map of Lewes

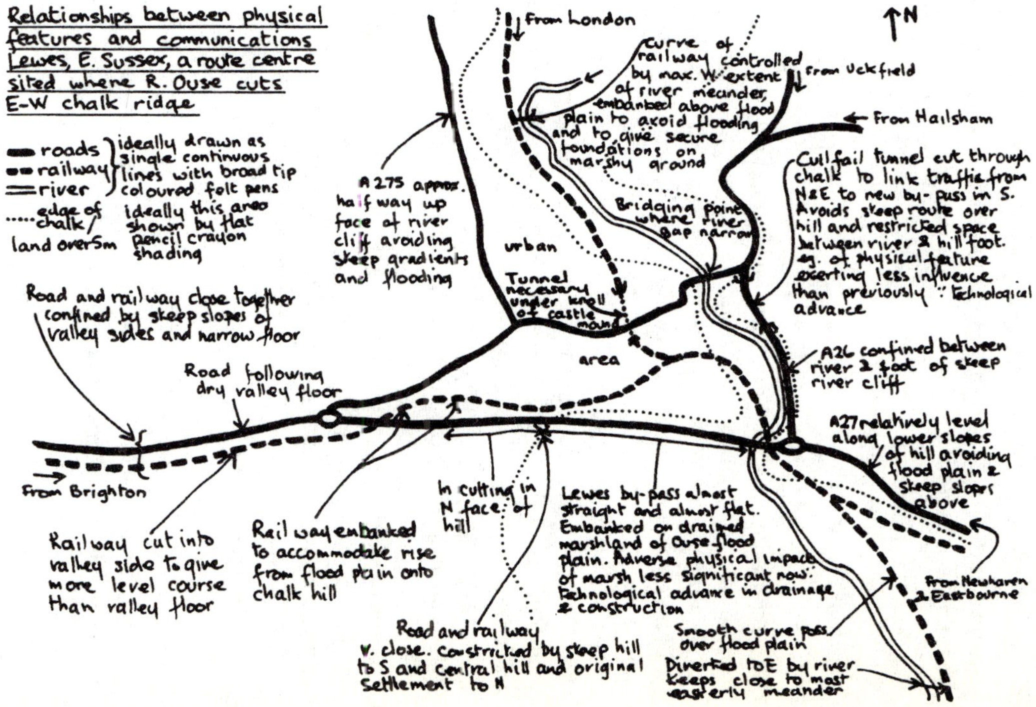

Patterns

Tony Buzan has developed a method of note-making called patterns. A pattern on the US political system, made up on Buzan lines, is shown opposite. A pattern is a web spreading out from a topic written in the centre of the page. Related ideas are printed on lines drawn from the topic. If you make a pattern, it is useful to remember these pointers:

(a) Keep it simple – try to write only two words per line.
(b) Print – it's clearer.
(c) Make your web lines from the box veer horizontally – it's easier to write on them.

You read a chapter, making light pencil marks against the key points if you own the book, or noting down page numbers if you don't, then you make your pattern and rub out the pencil marks.

In my experience, students' reactions to patterns vary. I have not found them as popular as the standard method for coping with notes. Many students do not like them at all. On the other hand, I have known patterns used in English Literature to good effect. I use them to sort out ideas which seem muddled or confused, sometimes making an ordinary, linear note afterwards. I also use patterns for shopping, where each 'arm' is a shop to be visited, and the 'branches' are things to be bought there. Material from more than one source can be combined on to one pattern, which is a strength; essays can be planned using them, each 'arm' of the web forming a paragraph, with the 'branches' being the content of the paragraph. Patterns structure material effectively.

Buzan's ideas can be followed up in the following books, which are interesting reading:

Buzan, T (1974) *Use Your Head*, London: BBC Publications.
Buzan, T (1977) *Make the Most of Your Mind*, London: Colt Books.

Buzan has made people more aware of the value of linking ideas by lines. A looser example is given overleaf.

A Buzan pattern-type note

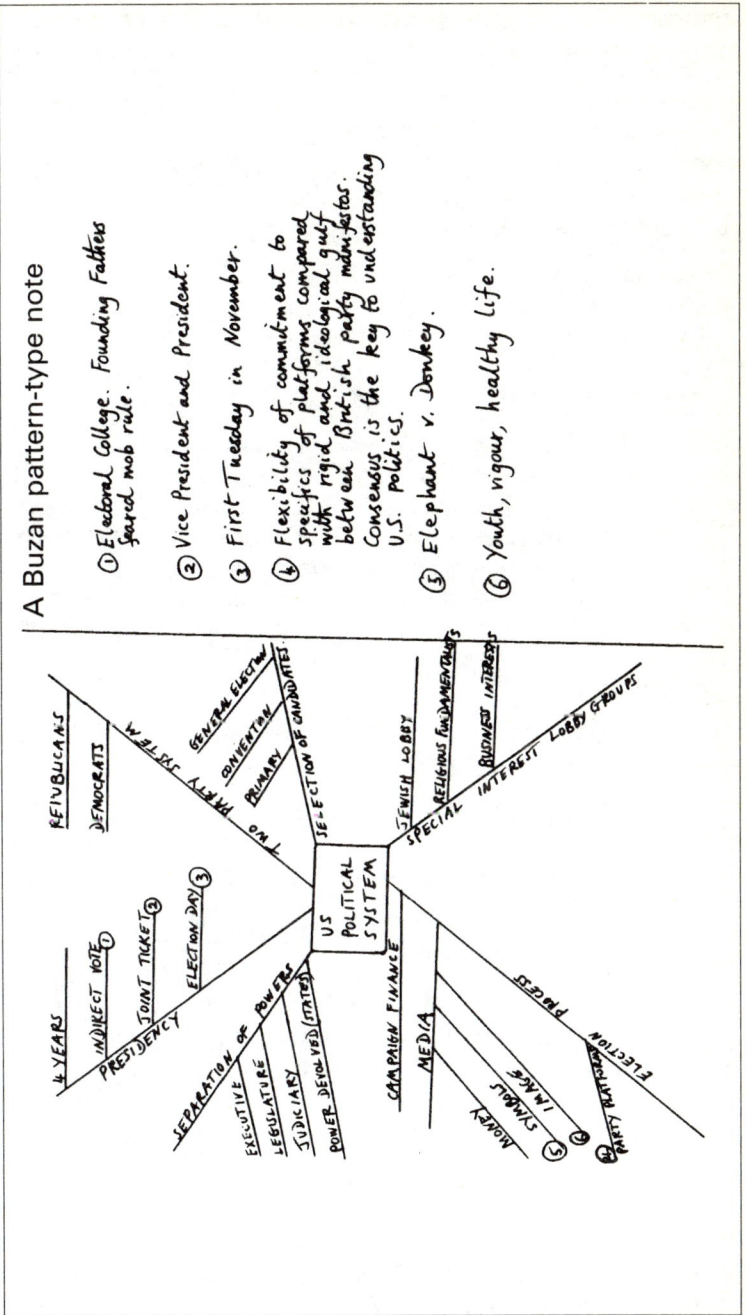

① Electoral College. Founding Fathers feared mob rule.

② Vice President and President.

③ First Tuesday in November.

④ Flexibility of commitment to specifics of platforms compared with rigid and ideological gulf between British party ministers. Consensus is the key to understanding U.S. politics.

⑤ Elephant v. Donkey.

⑥ Youth, vigour, healthy life.

Pattern-type diagram showing society in the coming age of leisure

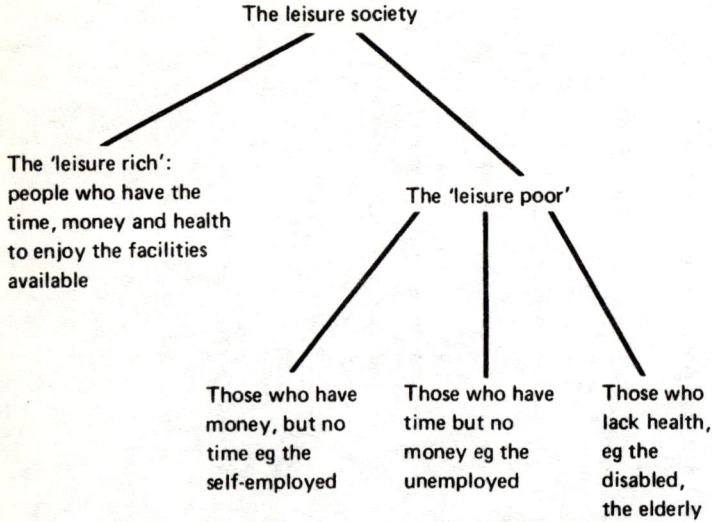

Underlining

If you *own* a book, and it needs to be mastered, underlining is a possibility. A method could be:

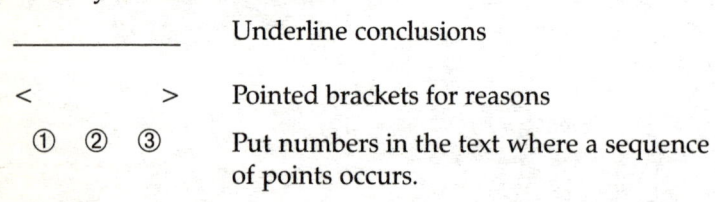

_____   Underline conclusions

<   >   Pointed brackets for reasons

① ② ③   Put numbers in the text where a sequence of points occurs.

Underlining is not popular. It is rather lacking in creativity, and your ideas on what is important may change. However, I have known it used very effectively to master a set book. The major drawback is that it stops you using your own words, which is so important in 'deep processing' material.

Flow charts

A flow chart is a diagram consisting of a series of geometric shapes connected by arrowed lines. Each shape has a special use. The oval denotes 'start' or 'end'; the diamond asks a question;

Flow chart for Psychology A Level analysing why a child may not be at school

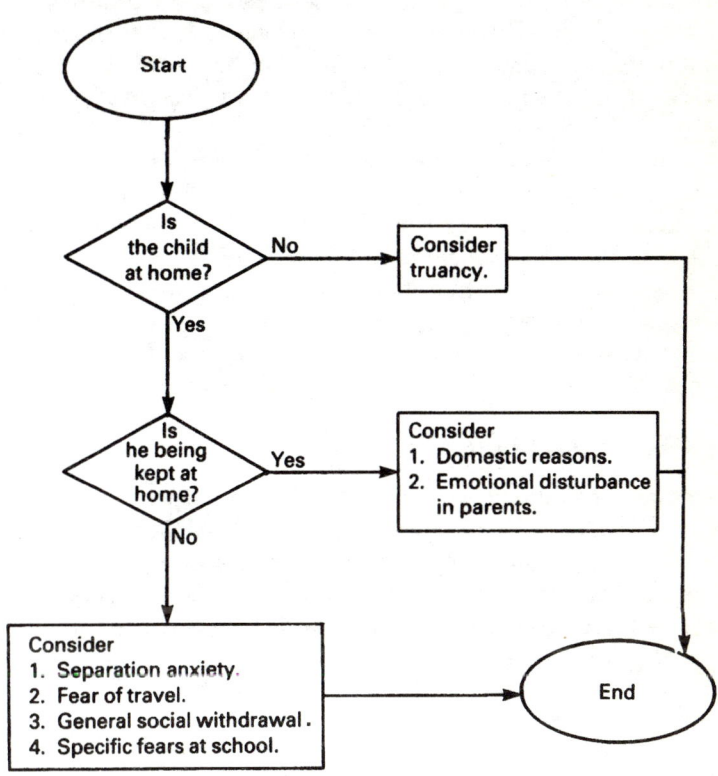

the rectangle does something. You will have met flow charts in your GCSE Mathematics, but they are useful in studying. They give a picture of how a procedure, system or sequence of events, operates. An example is shown above. I have used a looser example on p 143. When making flow charts, start in the top left-hand corner of the page, as the direction of the flow lines is down the page and from left to right. Keep the questions in the diamonds as simple as possible, and remember that each should have only two possible answers, yes or no. You will need flow charts in Advanced GNVQ Construction, for instance.

4.3 Using computers in note-making

Increasingly, students are making notes using computers. You can move information around very easily on a computer, so you should be able to achieve excellent structure and wording.

The problem is that you can see only one screen of information at a time, so it is more difficult to have an overview. Nor is it the best way to get an overview by becoming involved in very extensive moving around of material.

The key is to have some idea of structure before you use the computer. This involves skimming, reading and scanning exactly as discussed in 4.1; it is only at the last stage that you use the computer, instead of making notes on paper.

It is generally true that for any topic, there are between four and six major aspects. It is easier to work out what they are before you begin keyboarding.

4.4 Personal choice in notes

An example is shown on p 53 of a note on radioactivity made by a Physics A Level student who went on to read Dentistry at university. Numbering is not used, but there is a strong sense of layout, and the structure is readily apparent. The first side of the note is reproduced. I would prefer more use of space and a bigger diagram.

A note on radioactivity made by a Physics A Level student

Radioactivity.

Emission of radiation by a radioactive subst. is completely independent of temp. and pressure.

This radiation affects a photographic plate, causes gases through which it passes to ionize, and makes certain substances (eg crystalline zinc sulphide) fluoresce.

Types of Radiation.

Alpha Rays (α rays)

These are attracted to a negative plate and therefore carry positive charges.

Have been identified as helium ions $^4_2He^{2+}$, in rapid motion (identified spectroscopically).

Very little penetrating power.

Very strong ionizing effect on any gas through which they pass. (This property most useful for detection and measuring their intensity).

Beta Rays (β- rays)

Attracted to positive pole $\therefore$ carry a -ve charge. Beta particles (ie e^- or β^-) are electrons in very rapid motion (mass $= \frac{1}{1836}$).

About 100 times as penetrating as alpha rays.

However, much less effective in ionizing gases.

Gamma Rays (γ- rays)

Unaffected by an electric field $\therefore$ carries no charge. Gamma radiation is electromagnetic radiation of very high frequency. Resemble X rays but have an even shorter wavelength. Very great penetrative power.

Chapter 5

Writing Essays

Everyone has been taught at some time or other how to write an essay, and you may wonder what else there is to learn. In fact, almost everyone can improve their essay writing.

5.1 The features of a good essay

A good essay must have the following four features; without them, no essay can be good. The features are:

1. *A direct answer to the question.* The essay must address the issues that the question raises. Personal spark and personal conviction must be shown in giving your direct answer.
2. *The use of argument and evidence.* A case must be argued, and must be proved by precise, high-quality evidence.
3. *Effective organisation of material.* Rambling answers can never score high marks, even when the material is high quality.
4. *A clear and economical style.* No flim-flam.

In other words, you need a direct, lively, personal response to the question, well supported by evidence, clearly structured and clearly expressed.

People say they know this. But do they do it? One candidate didn't for her Oxford entrance, though she went on to get three grade As at A Level. The feedback was: 'She showed considerable energy but did not construct an argument of her own … She did not stop to think and consequently did not really answer the questions she chose.' Even more poignantly, an examiner wrote of an A Level examinee: 'It seems almost tragic that an apparently intelligent candidate (to judge by her style) should so disadvantage herself by an apparently wilful disregard of the terms and requirements of the question.'

You need a method to ensure that you deliver the four essential features.

5.2 How to produce a good essay

1. Realise that you must concentrate not on the *topic*, but on the *question* that you are asked about the topic

Take the title: 'Is cruelty a unifying theme in *Trois Contes*?' The topic is cruelty; the question is cruelty *as a unifying theme*.

Put the specifics of the question in the front of your mind. Look over your material on the topic, then filter it, select it and adapt it to fit the specific focus of the question. You have to pick the right bits of what you know, and put them to work on the question. The pattern of your thinking in addressing the question is more important than how much you know about the question.

Give a direct answer. Trust your judgement. Your essay must leave a definite impression of where you stand on the specific question asked: an excellent but balanced answer cannot get the top grade. Confidently dismiss wrong theories, giving your reasons and evidence.

2. Write rough notes on your arguments and evidence

You want arguments and evidence: not viewpoint, not assertion, not speculation, not description.

Write brief notes on your arguments and evidence, using your file to help you. Make precise statements supported by specific evidence: precision and proof are the hallmarks of scholarship. Develop your points. Beware of making unsupported generalisations.

3. Now structure your initial ideas before you write

Beware your first paragraph. Too often essays begin with a 'throat-clearing' introduction which says little, or with an 'hors d'oeuvre' introduction, which is better, but as it merely gives some interesting background or a quotation, does not go to the heart of the answer. Also, no 'defensive' starts such as: 'In order to answer this question, it is first necessary to . . .' and no 'traditional' introductions, in which you say how you are going to tackle the question. All these lead you away from answering the question. You end up feeling your way towards your answer as you write, with the considerable risk of diverging from the question.

The most important single point in essay-writing is to answer the question in the first paragraph. You are giving a generalised, direct answer – the core of your answer. You are putting your conclusion up front. In thriller terms, you're saying 'whodunnit'. If the essay ended after the first paragraph, it should be clear what your answer is. Conviction at the start carries power.

The 'nutshell' answer in the first paragraph confers two large advantages. First, you know where you're going. You are forced to be relevant, no mean feat, as more candidates are unsuccessful (or fail to fulfil expectations) through irrelevance, than for any other single reason. Second, the reader knows where you're going. This is a considerable help to him, like a map on which he can see his journey.

In the second paragraph, you should if necessary challenge any assmumptions in the question and define any terms which call for definition.

The evidence comes in the middle paragraphs. You need about four to six of them, each dealing with an aspect of the question. You should be able to say what that aspect is. The paragraphs should be in a logically developing sequence. The quickest way to convey disorganisation is: no paragraphs, or very short paragraphs.

The last paragraph is fresh reflections on 'whodunnit'. Not the tired 'In conclusion . . .'. Not a rehearsal of all the main points. Saying 'whodunnit', giving the evidence, and then giving fresh reflections in the conclusion, is *not* the same as the heavy-handed approach of 'say what you are going to say, say it, and say that you've said it'.

There is no right length for an essay, but very long essays are not often of high quality. You should be able to say everything necessary in not more than five sides of normal handwriting. In other words, as a guide, 650–800 words should be ample.

4. Write clearly

You are selling yourself on paper. Your handwriting must be clear and legible. Avoid the 'take it or leave it' attitude, as if to say: 'This is how I write and how I choose to spell – it's your job to make the best you can of it.'

Watch your syntax (eg, would of); no colloquialisms (eg, a loner, pushes his luck); no vogue words (eg, charisma, traumatic); no spelling errors (eg, definate, tradgedy).

Punctuate properly. The comma denotes a light pause, and should not become an 'all-purpose' punctuation mark. Make meaningful use of the colon and semi-colon (the colon means 'that is to say', and the semi-colon stands in place of a full stop, to join sentences which have some bearing on each other). Use apostrophes to mark possession; watch the difference between its and it's; and indicate titles of books by underlining.

Change your conception of essay writing: you're not *writing an essay on something*, you're *answering questions in essay-type format*. Avoid conventional, formal essays with elaborate introductions and conclusions.

5.3 Examples of a good essay

There follows an essay on Shakespeare's *Richard II*. It will repay careful study. Don't be put off by it: you can still do extremely well without reaching its excellent standard.

Notice how the answer is given in the first paragraph, and is re-stated in the conclusion. Notice how each middle paragraph deals with an aspect of the question – you will be able to see what each aspect is. Also, each middle paragraph makes reference to before and after Ireland, and is thus tightly relevant. The style is clear and economical, and arguments are supported by evidence from the text. The essay is a direct, personal response which leaves a clear answer in your mind.

'Richard is greatly changed after his return from Ireland.' Do you agree or disagree with this statement? Give your reasons.

Answer in 'nutshell' form.	I disagree most emphatically with the statement that Richard seems a different man after he returns from Ireland. It is true that superficially his behaviour shows marked differences, but that is only because the situation has changed in a marked way. He is the same man adapting himself in the same way to an environment that has become totally different. The changes are all in his circumstances, not in himself.

Self-dramatisation	The most marked thing about him is his self-dramatisation. He cannot help play-acting. Before he went to Ireland he acted the part of an all-powerful king, though he was really a weakling and surrounded himself with flattering favourites to keep up his ego. When he returns and finds he has lost his kingdom, though his grief is real enough, he plunges whole-heartedly into his new rôle – that of the martyr-king, unjustly humiliated. At the great deposition scene he acts everyone, including the victorious Bolingbroke, off the stage.
Hesitancy and uncertainty	Another characteristic is his hesitancy and uncertainty, always covered by some high-sounding speech. In the very first scene, where all authority is his, he orders Bolingbroke to drop his quarrel with Mowbray, and when Bolingbroke refuses Richard is baffled as a king, but not as an actor. He cries:

We were not born to sue, but to command.

But he gives way all the same. Then he begins to hesitate, and keeps on changing his mind. They shall fight at Coventry. At the last moment he stops this, and tries to evade the issue by banishing both. He behaves exactly in the same way on his return from Ireland, alternating between optimism and pessimism at every breath of bad news or word of encouragement, and at length yields abjectly to Bolingbroke at Flint Castle, but covering it as of old with a superb speech:

Down, down I come, like glistering Phaeton.

Treachery	There were worse things too than these, committed before he went to Ireland – his part in the murder of Gloucester, his misrule of England for the sake of his own pleasure for which John of Gaunt rebuked him, and his treacherous robbery of the latter's property. He naturally had no power to repeat these after his return, but the will still seems to have been there. He tries at the end of the deposition scene to buy a reprieve by suggesting that he should be allowed to retain the crown for his lifetime, and proclaim Bolingbroke the heir to it:

Cousin, I am too young to be your father,
Though you are old enough to be my heir.
What you will have, I'll give, and willing too.

Having seen his former acts of treachery, we can guess what would have happened if Bolingbroke had been foolish enough to let him have power again.

Charm   Yet with all his faults Richard certainly had charm, and this is as evident after as before he went to Ireland. His young wife, his favourites, the gardener, and his groom who went to see him in prison, all seem in their different ways to be devoted to him. The Duke of York, although he knows all his faults only too well, is with difficulty brought to join the other side, and weeps at his deposition. And in spite of his crimes and his play-acting, few members of an audience can see that deposition through without feeling some sympathy for the fallen king.

Answer restated   To return to the question, I consider that this review of Richard's character shows that it goes through no change in Ireland: the same vain, foolish, sometimes wicked, but none the less charming and pathetic young man as set forth, returned.

Also reproduced are the first, second, fourth and sixth paragraphs of an essay on T S Eliot written by a grade A English Literature A Level student in the actual exam. It is common to indent quotations so they stand out from the main body of the essay; here there is very close reference to the text but it is interwoven into the main body of the essay. The structure of the essay is:

1st para	Answer in nutshell form.
2nd para	The poem 'The Love Song of J Alfred Prufrock'.
4th para	The poem 'The Waste Land'.
6th para	Answer restated.

Part of grade A English Literature
A Level essay on T. S. Eliot

'The occasional obscurity in Eliot's early poems is an important part of their effect.' What is your own view?

1st para   T. S. Eliot in his early poems makes far greater use of a technique which he later tended to abandon in favour of conveying the pure power of words themselves. This is the technique of using references to other poets or writers, even quoting directly from them, and references to myth or religion. Naturally, but for the initiated, those (and they must be few) with a scholarly knowledge equal to Eliot's own, his poems must seem obscure and sometimes incomprehensible. These references are, however, an important and intrinsic part of Eliot's poetry. Through them, he provides parallels or contrasts to the present, about which he is writing.

2nd para   'The Love Song of J. Alfred Prufrock' is built upon such references and images, although it has not the obscurity of parts of 'The Waste Land', which shows the culmination and climax of Eliot's use of this technique. Prufrock is a lonely man, isolated in a society which has debased its spiritual values, where people have become less than people, merely 'arms' or 'skirts that trail along the floor'. The epigraph is taken from Dante who influenced Eliot profoundly and the literary works upon which it is based are Marvell's 'To His Coy Mistress' and 'Hamlet'. Marvell's poem stresses continually the fleeting, transitory nature of time, and the need to squeeze all possible experience out of life. Prufrock, by direct contrast, has not 'the strength to force the moment to its crisis', his indecision is that of Hamlet, and his eternal cry is 'Indeed there will be time', even though he has seen 'the eternal footman hold my coat and snicker' and fears death. He can never attain the vitality and decision of

Marvell, and neither is he 'prince Hamlet nor was meant to be', for he is no romantic hero, and Hamlet finally did 'force the moment to its crisis', and attained those heights of tragedy which are denied to Prufrock. These literary references are of vital importance to the effect of the poem. They compare a past age with the emptiness of the present, compare vitality and meaning (especially Marvell) with a depleted mankind.

4th para   'The Waste Land' is the climax of this technique. It is based on a framework of Shakespeare's 'The Tempest', and various references to ancient myths and fertility rites, particularly the legend of the Holy Grail, all of which hint at a possibility of rebirth and restoration. 'The Waste Land' is obscure, but the thoughts which Eliot is trying to convey are obscure and complex. Certainly the method can have its disadvantages. Sometimes Eliot's poetry is totally incomprehensible, and sometimes he seems to be enjoying academic 'in-jokes'. But in 'The Waste Land' the method gives unity to a long poem. Again the past contrasts with the sordid and depleted present. The 'sweet Thames' of Spenser's time is now reduced to a 'dull canal'. People, as in the preludes, are become bestial or inanimate, while objects and beasts take on human characteristics. The references give form to the poem, and hint continually at the possibility of redemption and restoration through faith, and willing surrender into it. The end of the poem is totally obscure, being a confusion of quotes and references, all of which still hint at the ultimate possibility of redemption although this has not yet been achieved. 'The Waste Land' without its network of reference and allusion would scarcely exist. It is given a rich and meaningful texture. The references provide contrasts with the present, and hint at the possibility of future redemption.

6th para   The obscurity of Eliot's poems can be considerable, but it is an important part of what he is trying to communicate. Reference and myth provide parallels and contrasts with the chaos and emptiness of modern living, and also give structure to the poems. The obscurity simply of language reflects the fact that it is often 'impossible to say just what I mean', that words are inadequate to express some of our deepest ideas and feelings.

Chapter 6

Other Essentials

The essentials of communication are vital both for GNVQs and for A Levels. For GNVQs, the core skill Communication mentions that grammar, punctuation and spelling should follow standard conventions, and the A Level boards have a code of practice which states that in your prose writing, marks awarded will take into account the quality of language used.

6.1 Good English

What is good English? Good English refers to a way of writing which gives your intended reader the best possible chance of understanding exactly what you mean.

How do you write good English? The Plain Language Commission argues that you need clear, crisp writing, with a good average sentence length (say 15–20 words throughout the document) and plenty of active voice verbs ('Bolingbroke deposed Richard' uses an active verb; 'Richard was deposed by Bolingbroke' uses a passive one). Your writing should be free from pomposity, using mainly everyday language. If your written work is really hard to understand, keep your sentences short, simple and human. Reading your work aloud will also help you to modify it.

A good book to consult is: Dummett, M (1993) *Grammar and Style for Examination Candidates and Others*, London: Duckworth. There is an excellent short section on spelling at the back of Ridout, R (1980) *The Pan Spelling Dictionary*, London: Pan Books.

6.2 Handwriting

Bad handwriting tires an examiner or an assessor, and makes it hard for him to grasp your work as a whole. Checking up on, and improving, handwriting is not as hard as one might think.

Of the specimens shown opposite, (b) is easier to read than (a) because it is closer to print. Most of what we read is print, and handwriting that approximates to print is thus easier to read.

However, we are not printing machines – we cannot write exactly like print: in the specimens, (c) is the printed alphabet, and (d) is a hand-written alphabet based on it, but with a few changes to make it easier for the hand. The a, g, k and y are different, for example, and the letters tend to be oval and leaning to the right. They are grouped according to formation. The closer your handwriting is to them, the better.

It is best to concentrate on two or three letters and improve them. A friend can isolate the most important ones for you. Most difficulties arise because one letter looks like another, and improvement in two or three letters can make a big difference. If you are practising a letter, practise the whole group in which it stands.

Alternatively, it may be that one important characteristic needs attention; for example to carve out the letters more, or to write smaller (smaller writing, but not too small, is easier to read).

Legibility is greatly assisted if you ensure that letters occupy all the zones they should. For instance, 'i' is only middle zone, 'p' is middle and lower zones, and 'h' is middle and upper zones. Make sure that ascending strokes really do go up, and that descending strokes really do go down.

6.3 Delivering a talk

Delivering a short talk is becoming more important. You may encounter this in A Levels, and it is important in GNVQs, where a talk may be given to an unfamiliar audience such as managers from the local business community.

1. Preparing the talk

The first thing is to structure what you have to say. If it is an 'informative talk', the structure is: create *interest*, give an *outline*

Specimens of handwriting

(a) *"The poetry of Dylan Thomas has no social reference or relevance." Discuss.*

If sex, decay and death are ~~not~~ not social subjects ~~are~~ or relevant, then the above statement is true. Most people automatically think that the ~~the~~ word "social" is a synonym for "political" which, of course, it is not. However, as the term "social" in-

(b) <u>**What part did Strafford play in the personal rule of Charles I ?**</u>

Thomas Wentworth, Earl of Strafford was the greatest minister of Charles I. He belonged to an old and wealthy Yorkshire family and was educated at St. John's College, Cambridge. He entered

---

(c) a b c d e f g h i j k l m n
     o p q r s t u v w x y z

(d) itl/nmrhbpk/uy/cad
     gqoe /vw vw/fjs/x/z

of what you will cover, make your points – *exposition* – and give a *summary*. For a 'persuasive talk', the structure is: ATTENTION, PROBLEM, SOLUTION, APPEAL.

Use brief notes on an index card (or cards). Use colour on the card but *don't write out the talk in full*, though you may write out the first and last sentences. Always try to have *three* headings in the main body of your talk.

Example:

```
ATTENTION:        in a crash,
                  your body is like a peach,
                  the car is like a hammer.
PROBLEM:          500 lives
SOLUTION:         'Seat belts for safety'

1.  They stop X happening
              ...
              ...
              ...
2.  They stop Y happening
              ...
              ...
              ...
              ...
3.  They stop Z happening
              ...
              ...
              ...

APPEAL:           WEAR ALWAYS
```

2. When waiting to deliver your talk

Remember the following maxim: 'I'm glad I'm here; I'm glad you're here; we'll get it together; I know that I know.'

3. Delivery

After your talk, you will answer questions. That will be your natural style. Use that style in your talk. Think of it as *dramatic conversation*.

Hold your card up in one hand, and keep it up. Use the other hand for gestures. Look at the card, then talk, don't look at your card and talk at the same time. Remember, a talk is dramatic conversation. Speak to the back.

GNVQs stress the importance of using visual images to support your talk. Use slides for pictures, never for print (you can't see it). Make only one or two points per slide. Overhead transparencies can be used for bold graphs, large diagrams or key words. When actually using a visual image, look *mainly* at your audience, not at the image (watch the weather announcers on TV). Display visual material only at the point when you want the audience to look at it.

Things to avoid: lecterns, mannerisms, swaying, shuffling your feet, locking your eyes on the floor or the ceiling (you want eye contact with the audience).

6.4 Business letters, memos, schedules

1. Business letters

A typical layout for a business letter is shown below:

```
                                    12 Regent Close
                                    Bridgetown
                                    TN20 6QZ

Mr H Barlow
20 Harbour Road
Bexbourne
BN12 1TZ


19 June 1994


Dear Mr Barlow

I enclose as requested some details of my work as a
hotel manager; apologies for the delay in responding
to your call.

Yours sincerely

[signed]

John King
```

Notice that you work from the left margin, starting with the receiver's address, apart from the sender's address which is top right above it; the month of the date is by name not number; 'Dear Sir' ends 'Yours faithfully', but if the person is named, you end 'Yours sincerely'. Only the main body of the text is punctuated.

2. Memos

A typical layout for a business memo is shown below:

```
To          Jane Smith
From        Emma Jones
Date        19 May 1994
Subject     Hotel and Catering Careers Seminar
_____

Just to let you know that this will now take place on
Tuesday 12 July 1994.
```

Note that it is not strictly necessary to sign a memo, but that To, From, Date and Subject are essential.

3. Schedule

The layout of a schedule is less well known, but here is a typical example:

```
VISIT TO THE HOTEL AND CATERING CAREERS SEMINAR
PALACE HOTEL, WESTMOUTH


Tuesday 12th July 1994


0930      depart      college by minibus

0945      arrive      Palace Hotel

1000                  Talk on the hotel industry by Mr
                      J Peter, Manager, Palace Hotel

1100                  Coffee, Main Dining Room

1120                  Series of talks in the Main
                      Reception Room: Food Service,
                      Housekeeping, Food Preparation

1220      depart      Palace

1245      arrive      college

Distribution:         all students on Adv GNVQ
                      Hospitality and Catering
```

Chapter 7
Time and A Levels

7.1 Time and revision

Throughout our discussion on time, one theme will keep emerging: the need for revision. Much of our learning is lost because of lack of revision, and the reason that we can recall languages more than other school knowledge is because, while learning them, words and constructions are being revised automatically all the time. There is a tragic pattern: students spend hours gathering material; near the exam they find that there is too much to learn so they cut out some; they then see questions on the exam paper which they could have answered if they had learned all their notes. Revision throughout the course will avoid this sad sequence.

The student who has the most passes at the top grade has five A Levels and three S Levels. He is in the *Guinness Book of Records*. His 'secret' was:

> 'Start revising early and remember it is a lot easier to learn over a long period than trying to cram at the end.'

He also worked hard:

> 'I guess I was also very introverted then and spent two or three hours a night doing homework.'

But spaced revision was the key to his success.

FIRST YEAR

7.2 The first term of A Levels

When people start their A Levels, there is usually a spate of eager activity: books are bought; equipment is bought; effort is expended. Some of the effort is wasted on work which quite soon is seen not to have been necessary, and the intensity of work drops, not to rise again until nearing the last third of the course.

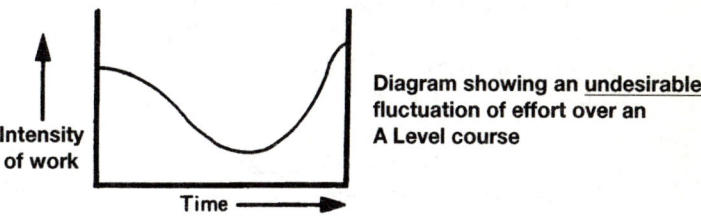

Diagram showing an <u>undesirable</u> fluctuation of effort over an A Level course

A better pattern is to have smaller fluctuations of effort over the duration of your course.

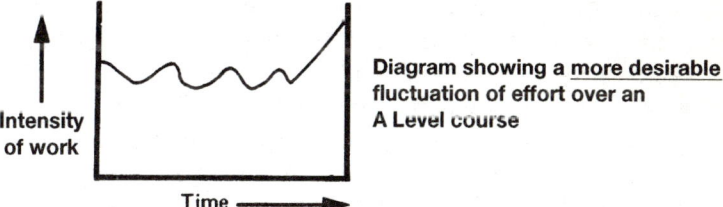

Diagram showing a <u>more desirable</u> fluctuation of effort over an A Level course

Throughout the whole of your course, always be sure you spend your time *on what is important*. Do not waste time by doing too much at the beginning and not enough in the middle of your course. Make sure you use the best books and that you deploy your time on what is really important. You need – from the out-set – three things to ensure your effort is well directed: plenty of past questions; some examiners' reports on past examinations; and the syllabus. And that is probably the order of their useful-ness to you. Buy these now. Use them for every topic you cover throughout your course. Always consult them before beginning any topic. You then clarify the target of your study.

7.3 Getting work done during term time

The first task is to establish your time blocks during which you will work as a habit. Habit is vital. Once something is established as a habit, it becomes easy, like eating three meals a day. It is actually two time blocks which you have to establish. The main one is to work from 7 to 9 pm each weekday evening, with 10 minutes' break in the middle. The subsidiary one is to work one other hour during each day, and to decide now exactly which hour on which day, for each weekday. This gives 15 hours during the working week. You should work at the weekend as well, for one two-hour session. Saturday morning is a good time, or failing that, Sunday evening. This gives in all 17 hours a week: that is about right as a norm, though you will go above and below this at times. The process described could be called 'landscaping' one's time.

Having established your time blocks, there are three pointers to help you get work done during term time:

1. *For written work, start early and finish early*, doing one assignment at a time. Starting early is often a problem: it is all too easy to leave beginning until too near the date on which the work has to be handed in. Procrastination rituals are undertaken ... that is to say, there is always something which seems (mistakenly) more important. But don't procrastinate. Start early: written work needs mulling over. Equally, aim to finish early: aim to finish before the handing-in deadline. Then, if anything occurs to delay you, you have some time in hand.

   Also, focus on one assignment at a time, and stick with it until you finish it. You then feel you have made progress. Do not flit from one assignment to another, or you will be continually 'picking up the threads' of your thinking. I feel this is an extremely valuable principle.

2. *For learning work, start early and finish late*. As soon as you know you have a test, make a revision note. This is not the final revision note you will use before A Levels: it can be thrown away. It is a temporary aid but it establishes the habit of using revision notes, as well as helping you learn for the test in hand. At the beginning of each learning session, look over the entire note. Within the note, master one small 'cell' at a time. Repetitions (which usually take the form of reading over the material) should alternate with acts of recall. It is

safest to look immediately if you cannot remember, to avoid implanting guesses in your mind. Learning is best done in small bursts which are spread over as long a period as possible. Thus, for learning work, start early and have short sessions spaced out right up to the time of testing.

3. *For all work, say to yourself: 'By X o'clock I will have done Y amount of work.'* Then, after a short period, see how you are getting along. Always have a target when you sit down to work: know how much you are going to achieve in a work session, otherwise you work in a drifting fashion.

7.4 Consolidating work during term time

Once your teacher has completed a unit of work in class, you should revise this. Such 'immediate revision' is immensely valuable. It clears up any difficulty while the topic is still fresh, and clarifies the material, bringing it into sharp focus. You can see the topic as a whole, and viewing it in this way can shed new light. Things fall into place. The Saturday two-hour work session discussed in section 7.3 is a good time for this recapping process. You can get away with not doing this 'immediate revision'; no one will check, unless it coincides with a test. But it is wise to make post-topic recapping a matter of policy.

7.5 The Christmas holiday

During your first term you should have been doing immediate revision, that is, looking over work when it has just been covered. Tests will have encouraged you to do this. During this holiday, it is necessary to do some maintenance revision, ie go over your first term's work. It is not easy to do this during the Christmas holiday: there is Christmas; there is the New Year. But it is very important to consolidate your first term's work over the Christmas holiday. Imagine there is a big test on the first day of the Spring term.

7.6 Spring term

Make sure your effort does not 'dip': remember the first diagram on p 71. One way to maintain your drive is to start thinking what you are going to do when you leave. True, you have another year of your A Levels after this one, but it soon goes and careers thinking must begin now.

7.7 Spring holiday

This is so often wasted by first year students. Of course you must consolidate your Spring term's work, but the key job this holiday, once that is done, is to prepare for the end-of-year internal examinations. These examinations can be used as practice for your A Levels, and you should practise preparing. Again, pretend that you have a big test when you go back for the summer term, and get revision notes together on all your work so far. This is excellent practice in making revision notes. Usually people find it best to do a final set of revision notes beginning at Christmas in their second year, when the work can be seen with the benefit of extra maturity and experience, but these revision notes could be a guide.

You will have little time during the summer term to prepare for your end-of-year internal examinations: staff have syllabuses to cover and will not give you much revision time. Lack of preparation in the spring holidays will mean either pressure or a poor shot at your end-of-year internal exams. Easter revision is the answer. Remember the highly successful student mentioned at the beginning of this chapter.

7.8 Dealing with mid-course lack of motivation

It can happen that motivation flags during the middle of your A Level course. The freshness of the start has gone; the urgency of the end has yet to come. Interest can wane. You have to consider other sources of propulsion. They are:

1. The realisation that A Levels are a *means to a desired aim*, for example:

    (a) getting into university
    (b) getting into a particular career
    (c) being 'a success'
    (d) making one's parents happy.

2. The sense of *felt achievement*:
    (a) really understanding something is a good feeling
    (b) getting a unit of work done in a set time makes you feel you are achieving something
    (c) doing well in a test is a big boost. Work very hard for any test.

All motivation comes down to a matter of need. If your motivation flags, you must answer the question, 'Why do I need to do this?' You will not be more motivated until you have specified this answer to yourself.

7.9 Summer term

Two things: try to do about half an hour's revision a day in preparation for your end-of-year exams (make it a habit to finish off your weekday evening study times with a bit of revision); and second, firm right up on careers thinking. Neither of these things is at all burdensome, but if you don't do them they will store up trouble for you in the future.

7.10 Summer holiday

You can have a really good break in the summer – and you should, for the coming year is going to be tough! But you have some tasks for the summer holidays: consolidate and go over your year's work, concentrating on any weaknesses; do wide reading, being guided by past questions and by examiners' reports; do some preparatory work on next year's syllabus as this will make the second year much easier.

SECOND YEAR

7.11 Autumn term

The pace hots up now. Beware of getting behind with your work. Get started on it as soon as it is set, and aim to finish well ahead of the handing-in time. Do not get to the end of the term with a backlog of work, for there are always extra events towards Christmas and you will find it harder then to finish assignments. Get your course applications off early, by half term at the latest (some need to go in earlier): this may increase your chances of acceptance, but in any case it decreases your anxiety and early offers will add to your motivation. If you are nervous about interviews, remember Winston Churchill's advice and imagine the interviewer is sitting in front of you in only his underpants.

7.12 The Christmas holiday

You will need to use this holiday well in order to prepare for the mock examinations in January: begin to make your final set of revision notes. Start on topics that are fully complete. The process of making final revision notes begins now and must be finished by the end of the spring holiday. You will have been referring to past questions and to examiners' reports throughout your course, but do so again now to check your coverage of a topic before making your final revision note on it. You cannot do revision notes on all your work for the mock exams, so do some quick, rough revision notes on the topics that cannot (because of lack of time or incompleteness of coverage) be finished now.

It is vital you plan your time over Christmas. People are often reluctant to do this. They make statements like: 'I can only work when I feel like it.' What they fear is the supposed limitation on freedom that they feel planning imposes. But planning saves a great deal of time in the long run: the total time to complete planned tasks is less than for unplanned tasks. And planning actually gives you more freedom: by telling you when you should be working, it also tells you when you need not be! What is needed is a simple but effective planning method.

The first thing is to '*landscape*' your time, ie decide the times of the day when you are going to work, a concept mentioned earlier. Occasionally students work to school times during the holiday, changing over subject matter when they would have changed subjects at school. This is one way, but it fragments your time, and you are better off concentrating on a topic or subject for longer than a term-time session. It is probably best to work from 10 am to 1 pm and from 7 to 9 pm, with 10-minute breaks from 50 minutes to the hour. As a generalisation, the afternoon is not such a good time to work following revision all morning, *but* there may well be people who find this their most productive time, and they should not be put off. As an alternative to the evening session, you could work from 4 to 6 pm for your second session.

The next stage is to *decide what to do when*. Having insisted on planning, one must now insist on avoiding over-planning! You need something simple and workable which will take best advantage of the holiday you have, which is very likely to be only some 14 days in total. I suggest compiling a diagram like the one overleaf.

There are one of two points to remember about this diagram:

1. *Weighting*. This method enables you to consider logically whether you wish to give one A Level more time than the others.
2. *A unit a day*. You do a complete unit of one A Level on one day: do not mix subjects. Each unit is as much as you could just about do in the morning alone, if you worked really hard and things went really well. The second session of the day is overspill time – or free as a reward if you really do finish as planned, though going over your day's work before sleeping is a good idea.
3. *Ticking days*. Every day is ticked as it passes: both the free ones and the work ones. You have the flexibility to choose what to do each day. Many people find that two days on the same subject is a good idea. Ticking days is a morale booster and a motivator.

It is best to see A Levels as being one full year followed by one full term and an extended period of exam build-up lasting the other two terms of the second year. This is how you could think of it: it may not correspond with how your teachers pace their courses.

7.13 Spring term

One hour a day should be given over to revision. Make it your final hour of evening study. I know you have fresh work to do, but remember the *Guinness Book of Records* student. Make time for one hour's revision a day during the week. A major aim is to carry on making your final revision notes. This should go on throughout the term.

How to plan holiday work

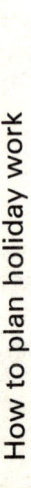

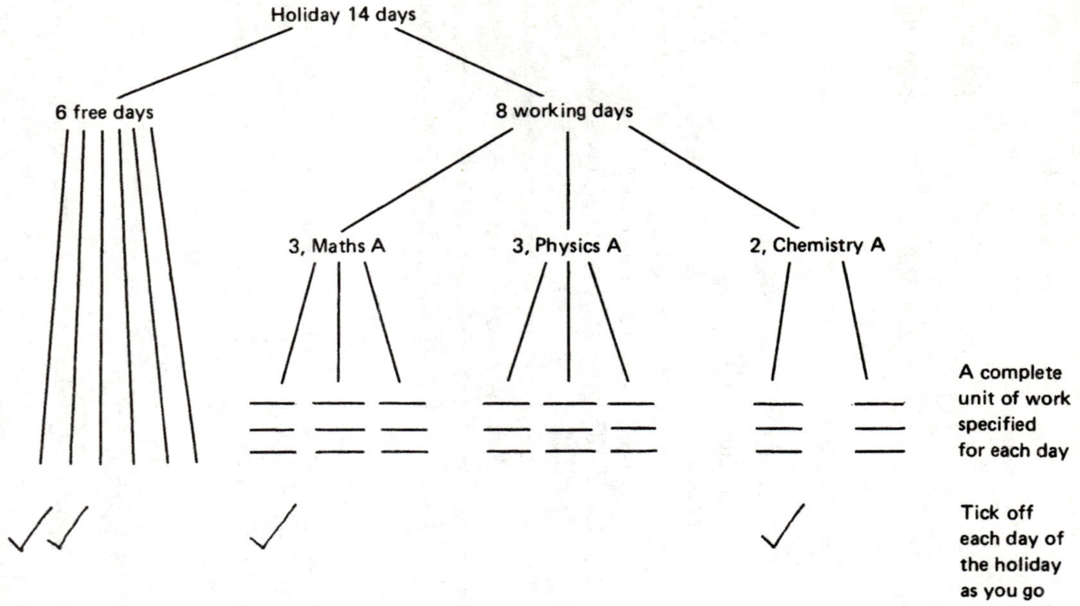

Holiday 14 days

6 free days

8 working days

3, Maths A

3, Physics A

2, Chemistry A

A complete unit of work specified for each day

Tick off each day of the holiday as you go

7.14 Spring holiday

Use the same holiday time planning method you used at Christmas (see section 7.12 on pp 76–77). This is a vital holiday. You must finish all your final revision notes by the end of it if you possibly can (remember to check with past questions and with examiners' reports to make sure your coverage is first rate in difficult areas). If you have any set books, you should now be reading them again and again: when you get to the end, go back to the beginning and start again. Knowledge of the text is much more important than anything else – and certainly much more important than critical works. Think of set books as a comprehension exercise: knowledge of the text is the most important requirement. This also includes firm memory of apposite quotations.

7.15 Summer term

You finished your revision notes by the beginning of this term (I trust) and now you have to keep going over them. Go over them again and again. Look at the note, then try to recall what is there. When you are stuck, look immediately to save sowing guesses in your mind. You must not just learn, but *over*learn your material so that you have it at your fingertips under the pressure of the exam room.

Any set books you have are treated in the same way: you keep reading them over and over again. Before sessions, it is a good idea to cast your eye over past questions and examiners' reports: A Level is gymnastics – you have to be able to move your knowledge around to fit a wide range of questions.

You may be given set revision by your teachers. There are two ways of dealing with this: either fit your own revision in with what is set, or do set work on weekdays before 7 pm, keeping weekday evenings and the weekend for your own revision. Students tend to prefer the latter policy. Also, I have noticed that many students find it a good idea to revise one A Level subject for three consecutive study sessions before changing to another.

Two don'ts. Try to avoid doing new work. You shouldn't need to anyway, but now is the time to consolidate, not to push out the boats. Second, don't cut out work, omitting to study it for the exam. Mass axing of material is the first step towards failing, and some students are tempted to 'spot' topics, and then cut out large chunks of their course. Look at it another way. Concentrate on key areas, giving them extra attention. They are bound to be on the question paper, and your smaller topics are easier to learn then because they fit into the key areas. Concentration on key areas can improve a mark by 10 per cent, but beware of leaving out material, for, apart from anything else, your teachers may have left out some of the course anyway. If you must spot (which is like gambling on the horses), do it as a fringe activity, very much as an extra 'on the side': just look over the last few papers (which is what the setter does). No elaborate statistical analyses. On the other hand, try to get some clues (from past papers and from examiners' reports) about what could turn up. Be 'cue seeking', not 'cue deaf'.

7.16 Modular A Levels

For some time now modular courses have been in existence in several universities, where they have proved popular. They are now emerging at A Level. This format allows you the opportunity to sit exams at times throughout your course, though a certain proportion of exams will still have to be taken at the end.

1. The good news about modular exams:

    (a) They motivate you to work hard sooner rather than later, so inoculating you against the mid A Level dip in effort.
    (b) You can take the exam shortly after you have been taught the work, while it's fresh in your mind.
    (c) You get formal feedback throughout your course, so you know where you stand.
    (d) You can re-sit modules and use your best results to make up your A Level grade.

    For these reasons, modularisation may raise your final result. All this will happen automatically. It's the things to watch that you need to remember.

2. Points to watch about modularisation:

    (a) *Stress*. Modularisation avoids the stress of a lot of final exams, but you have instead the stress of constantly sitting exams that count. The *remedy* is to start each piece of

work early, never to let things go if you don't understand, and to balance work with sport or other activities.

(b) *An impoverished lifestyle*. Often the worthwhile and
deeply rewarding activities (such as music or drama)
require a regular commitment of time. Concerts and
plays may well come close to module exam times. The
remedy is to plan ahead and organise your time, not axe
your activities. My own studies of university students
who get Firsts, indicate that they continue their activities
alongside their studies throughout their course.

(c) *Premature entry*. You may need more time to adjust to A
Levels from GCSE, bearing in mind that each module is
assessed at the full A Level standard, irrespective of
when you take it. Though you don't have to name modules or their results on your university application form,
these details could well come out, for instance in interview. The *remedy* in theory is not to enter until you're
ready, but you will be under the pressure of expectation
from your college and friends.

(d) *Re-taking modules*. Don't rely on re-taking modules. It's a
useful thing to be able to do, but it will interfere with
your studies. The *remedy* is to get a good result first time.

(e) *Safeguarding non-modular A Levels*. They run the risk of
being squeezed if you skew your effort. Remember that
you need a high and even level of achievement across
your A Levels. Non-modular subjects are likely to be
squeezed at the end of terms, when the modular exams
take place. The *remedy* is to work extra hard on them at
the beginning of the next holiday, pretending that there
is an exam in them at the beginning of the following
term.

These points to watch should not set you too much on edge.
Modularisation has come in successfully. The more familiar it
becomes, the fewer will be its problems. Because it enforces continuous learning, it probably promotes deeper learning.

Chapter 8

Time and GNVQs

An *overall time plan* is essential if you are going to complete your GNVQ. There is a lot to do. You need to know from the outset when you will be doing a unit, and how long you have to do it. Beware: some people do not finish their GNVQs. If your college does not insist on tight deadlines, make the commitment to yourself that you will finish a unit on time. Advanced GNVQs are basically a two-year course, but the boards don't insist that you finish within that time. Do not let this lure you into thinking that you have all the time in the world. In the early days, some colleges underestimated the time needed for GNVQs; if in doubt, check with your college that they and you are spending sufficient time.

The *use of time* in tackling an assignment is central to achieving a Distinction in your GNVQ. You can pass simply by satisfying the specifications, or syllabus, and by passing the external tests. But Distinction or Merit depend on whether you adopt the right approaches at the right time while you are doing your work: in other words, time and tasks are very closely linked. You cannot get a Distinction solely on the quality of your work. You must also approach your work in the right way, and you must satisfy your assessors and verifiers that you have done so. This means noting down how you go about your work, as this evidence will be required. The processes that you adopt when working are as important as the work you produce.

Apart from Quality of Outcome, there are three *grading themes* for your work if you are going to get a Distinction:

- Planning
- Information Seeking and Handling
- Evaluation.

It is essential that you become very familiar with these, so that you can judge your performance against them as you progress through the course. The following comments will help.

8.1 Planning

Before any planning starts, be very clear about the aim of your assignment.

1. *Drawing up plans of action.* You have first to break down your tasks into manageable steps. You must show that you are able to do this *by yourself*, and for *complex* tasks. You should organise visits yourself, and make a schedule for them, like the one on p 69; external visits for work experience are vital to GNVQs. Think through the consequences of your approach, and try to pre-empt problems. Estimate the time required for each step. You will now have all the steps or tasks numbered in order of *priority* from beginning the research to handing in the project. Now draw up your action plan. It can be quite simple. Indicate when you will do a task by using a shaded rectangular box as shown below:

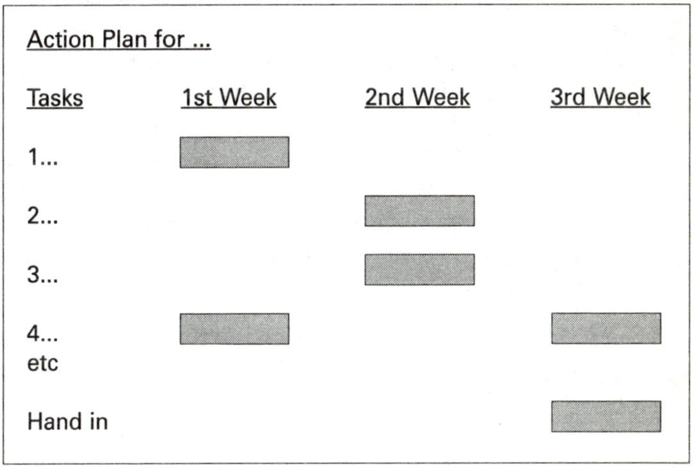
Action Plan for ...
Tasks
1st Week
2nd Week
3rd Week
1...
2...
3...
4...
etc
Hand in

2. *Monitoring courses of action.* This involves recording developments as they happen. Again, do this *independently*. You have to check your progress against your plan, noting what goes well, but in particular, spotting when different action is

needed, in response to what is unexpected or unforeseen. The key is to spot whether, when and *how* to change your plan. You must record as you go:

Monitoring of Action Plan for...

Task	Date planned	Date actual	Time planned	Time actual	Comments
1. ...					
2. ...					

8.2 Information-seeking and handling

1. *Identifying and using relevant resources.* You should do this *on your own*. It is important to consider a wide *range* of information, eg books, visits, IT, tutors, interviews. Don't forget less obvious ones. Make sure that your range of resources is chosen to enable you to explore different slants on the topic. Choose the resources which relate directly to the task, say what you have used and why, and list your sources. It is important to justify your selection from a range.

2. *Establish the validity of your information.* A useful thing to ask yourself is: Who produced this, and why? A source can be reliable, or useful, for one thing and not for another. Choose yourself *what* needs to be checked and *how* it can be checked. Comparing sources helps. Again, be *independent*. See p 28 on bias, and on fact and opinion. You will need to comment on this.

Write up comments as you go. Have a title *Resources for assignment on...* and use the two subheadings above. Be sure your comments cover the areas indicated.

8.3 Evaluation

1. *Evaluating outcomes and alternatives.* Refer back to your original aim. Say what you learned. This is a time for reflection. How successful was what you did? Look at the plus and the

minus. Remember that your project can be successful from one point of view, but not from another. The crucial thing is to consider a range of alternative courses of action that could have been taken, and to discuss their likely outcome. How else could you have carried out the assignment? *Alternatives* must be *applied* to your project.

2. *Justify your approach.* Say why you did what you did. Mention the modifications you made. Were your resources adequate? You will now be in a position to say *how you would do it differently next time*.

Again, write up comments as you go. Have a title *Evaluation of assignment on...* and use the sub-headings indicated above.

A good deal of stress has been put on working independently, but this doesn't mean you should avoid your tutors like the plague. There is all the difference in the world between saying 'How do I do this?' (which is dependent) and 'This is what I have done, these are my ideas, this is what I plan to do – what do you think?' (which is independent). If you are stuck, ask, but try yourself first, then you have some feedback to take to your tutor. The key to independence is to put yourself in the driving seat, as opposed to expecting to be driven. Look again at p 27 to re-cap on how your relationship with your teacher is different from that at GCSE.

Chapter 9

A Level Coursework

Coursework is any activity which you carry out during your course and which is directly assessed as part of the actual examination. A number of A Levels and AS Levels now include coursework. The range of coursework is wide, from fieldwork and experimental laboratory work, to individual studies and collections of pieces of written work.

9.1 Three golden rules

In all coursework, you should:

1. Make sure you have the *precise details* from the examination board of what is required. These days, such details are freely available. Your teachers will have them. Ask. The comments in this chapter will be widely applicable, but should be tailored to the requirements of each piece of coursework, as stated by the board.
2. Learn from the *experience of others*. Seek the views of past students or of students in the year above you. Ask your teachers about the errors and strengths of previous coursework similar to yours.
3. *Start writing-up early*. At least a quarter of the time for a project should be allocated to drafting and amending the final version. This means you must begin work on your project as soon as it is set, to allow time for mulling it over and amending it at the end. It helps to do some writing up as you go along, if you can. In this way, it will not swamp your other work.

9.2 Choosing a topic

1. *A good topic interests you and the reader.* Your topic must provide you with sufficient interest to sustain long study, otherwise choose something else. But in addition, you must make your topic interesting for the reader. Surface devices like violence, catastrophe or the unmasking of a hero create interest, as does, on a deeper level, any topic which shows that something is not what it seems. The interesting is mid-way between the absurd and the obvious.

2. *The size must be right.* Beware too broad a topic. It is better to write a lot about a little, than a little about a lot. Narrow down your topic. For example:

    ■ The nuclear issue.
    ■ Nuclear power, not weapons.
    ■ The safety of nuclear power.
    ■ Has Chernobyl had an impact on the development of safe nuclear power in the United Kingdom?

    Be sure that the topic is not so narrow as to leave you with too few sources. This angle needs checking before you start.

3. *Questions make the best titles.* Your title must centre on a problem, preferably expressed as a question. Your choice of title is crucial in spurring you on to show what you can do. A problem expressed as a question gives you direction and purpose: you select, arrange and interpret material, rather than simply accumulate it. A problem that cannot be turned into a question is not a problem at all. The title 'Women in the novels of D H Lawrence' is not likely to produce as good a result as 'Does "O for a life of sensations rather than thoughts" truly reflect the nature of Keats's poetry?'

9.3 Doing the research

1. *Collecting material.* Read short, general material first, to acquire a feel for your topic, then move to longer, more detailed material. Start with modern books first, then use older ones as necessary. Sources can be recorded on 3×5 inch cards, and notes on 5×8 inch cards. In both cases, use only one side of each card; you can then easily move material around. Study the diagram on p 88 which gives examples of source and note cards.

Examples of source and note cards used for collecting material for projects

Source cards

A book

Jung C G (1940).

The Integration of the Personality.
London: Routledge and Kegan Paul.

An article in a book

Jacobs M (1984).

"Psychodynamic Therapy:the Freudian Approach".

In Dryden W (ed).
Individual Therapy in Britain.
London: Harper and Row.

An article in a journal

Jensen A R (1969).

"How much can we boost IQ and scholastic achievement?"

Harvard Educational Review, 39, p. 1 - 123

An article in a newspaper

Buxton N (1988).

"Into Africa with Jung".

Sunday Telegraph,
17 April,
p.79

An interview

Jones M J (1988).

Jungian analyst.

Interviewed 2 January.

Note card

DREAMS: WATER SYMBOLISM

Jung (1940), p.67

2. *Representing information*. Don't forget annotated diagrams (discussed on pp 45–46). Photographs could be useful in some cases. Graphs, bar charts and tables are the most effective ways of presenting numerical data. It is easy to underperform on them, hence they are on pp 89–92. Some of the points may seem basic, but they are often not done.

How to draw a good graph

Graphs are used to illustrate a trend. Follow the instructions and look at the example overleaf.

1. Use a sharp pencil.
2. Use graph paper.
3. Write the title of the graph.
4. Make a grid of the data.
5. Draw two axes at right angles to each other. Label the origin (the point at which they meet) '0' and put arrows on the ends of the axes.
6. Label each axis, and state the units near each label. Performance goes on the vertical axis.
7. Choose a suitable scale to use as much of the graph paper as possible. If there is a break in the scale on either axis, indicate it as follows:

How to show breaks in the scales of a graph

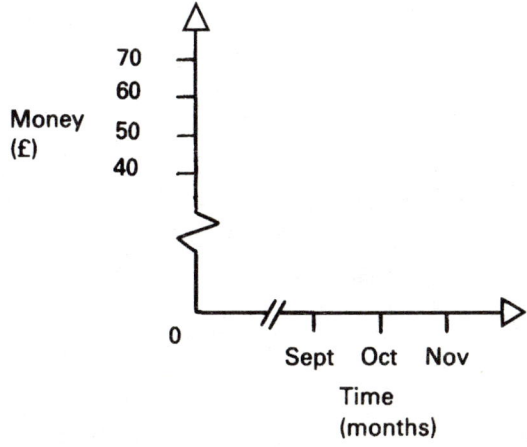

An example of a good graph

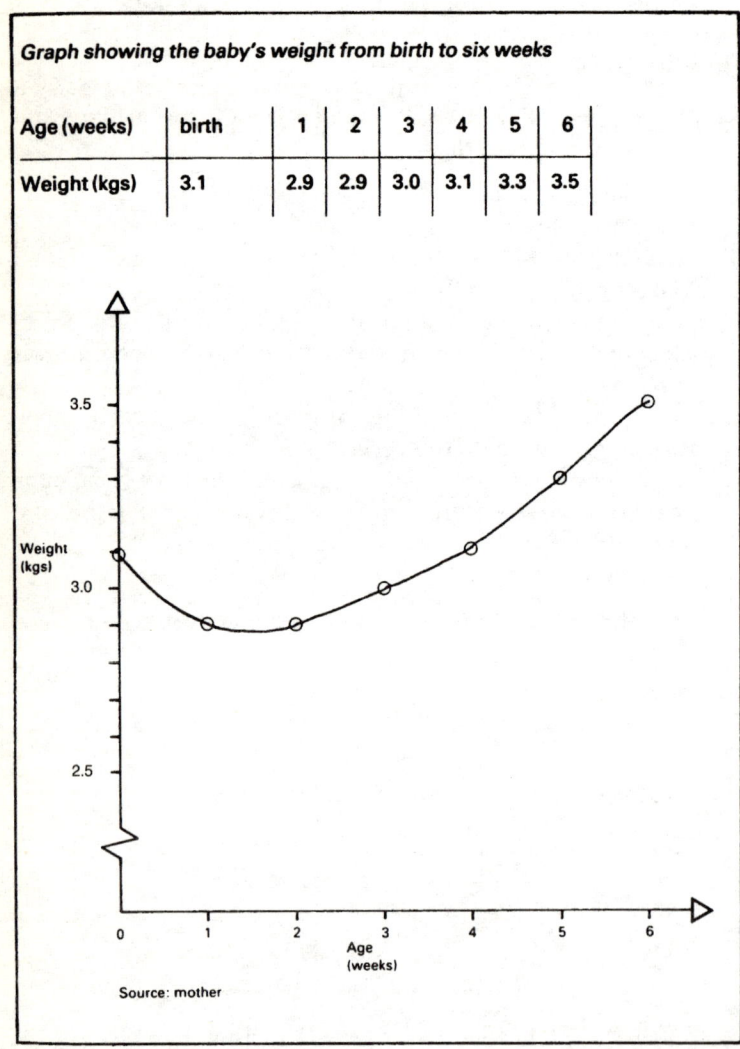

Graph showing the baby's weight from birth to six weeks

Age (weeks)	birth	1	2	3	4	5	6
Weight (kgs)	3.1	2.9	2.9	3.0	3.1	3.3	3.5

Source: mother

8. Plot each point with a dot in a circle: ⊙
9. Join the points with straight lines if the data is not continuous (eg, airline fatalities per month). Use a curved line if the data is continuous (eg, changes in room temperature).
10. Add the source at the bottom.

How to draw a good bar chart

Bar charts *compare separate items*. They are constructed similarly to graphs, but note that the axes do not have arrows. When drawing the bars, make them all the same width (4mm) keep them apart; and draw diagonal lines across them.

An example of a good bar chart

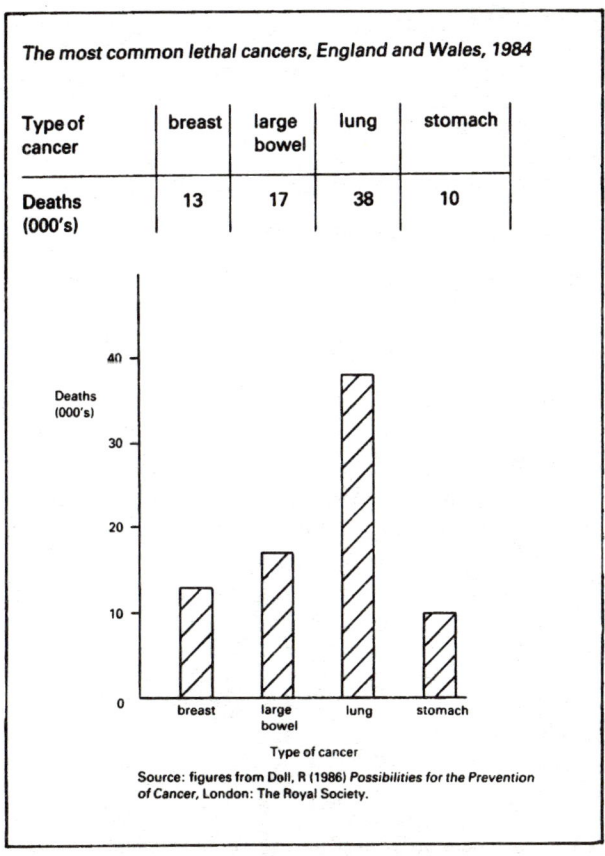

The most common lethal cancers, England and Wales, 1984

Type of cancer	breast	large bowel	lung	stomach
Deaths (000's)	13	17	38	10

Source: figures from Doll, R (1986) *Possibilities for the Prevention of Cancer*, London: The Royal Society.

How to make a good table

Tables show how a particular total is *divided up*. Use the one below as a model. Ensure that the table develops down, not across, the page.

An example of a good table

Motorists breath-tested during a two-week police campaign in Sussex, Christmas 1985	
Alcohol consumed	**Number**
Over the legal limit	220
Up to the legal limit	455
None	325
Total	**1,000**

Source: figures from local press

9.4 Writing up your study

1. *The title page.* See p 93 for a model, based on an imaginary case. A professional title page creates an excellent first impression.
2. *The contents page.* A simple layout is best, like the one on p 94. You should give the number and title of chapters, followed by their page numbers.
3. *List of illustrations.* All tables, maps and diagrams used in the study should be listed, with page numbers given.
4. *Introduction.* In this you should:

   (a) Explain why the problem is important.
   (b) State the aims of the study.
   (c) Discuss the methods of enquiry adopted.
   (d) Acknowledge help received, eg from librarians.

   It may be easier to write the introduction last.

An example of a title page

HOW FAR DID THE SECOND WORLD WAR AFFECT

DAILY LIFE IN EASTBOURNE?

by

Kathcrine Rachel Maya

A dissertation

submitted in partial fulfilment

of the requirements for A Level History

Joint Matriculation Board

June, 1994

An example of a contents page

CONTENTS

5. *The main chapters.* A4 wide-lined paper is a good size, or you can type on unlined A4 paper. A well-presented hand-written report receives no less credit, but it can be helpful if you type it.

   Special references to, or quotations from, books, articles or interviews should be cited, but do not cite general or background reading. Cite sparingly, using the following examples as a guide:

   > Jung (1940) describes ...
   > In her short study, Fordham (1959) discusses ...
   > In Brown's standard work on the post-Freudians (Brown, 1964) ...
   > Gross (1987, p 681) states that ...
   > In interview, Jones (1988) argued that ...

   Aim to keep within the word limit with a little to spare. If your study is too short, you probably haven't made, or critically developed, sufficient points; if it is too long, you have probably accumulated unnecessary material which you can edit out.

   Once you have done your first draft, put it aside for a day or so, then look at it afresh. Check not only the content, but also the English. Cross out unnecessary words. Eliminate vague subjects like 'it' or 'this'. Shorten long sentences or put in a comma so that the reader can draw breath. Read your project aloud to catch remaining errors in style.

   Remember to number the pages.

   Look out for a suitable soft-covered binder.

6. *Conclusion.* A general summary of what was found, including its significance and implications. Also mention problems and limitations.

7. *Bibliography.* All interviews and texts actually cited should be listed in alphabetical order of author, exactly as on your source cards, models of which are on p 88. For example: Jung, C G (1940) *The Integration of the Personality*, London: Routledge and Kegan Paul.

9.5 Experiments

Some points to watch in experiments are:

1. *Design.* In deciding on the procedure to be followed, consider at least two valid alternatives, then select the best.

2. *Apparatus.* You must develop the confidence to set up equipment unaided. Consciously plan for safety. Indicate in your report the safety measures taken.

3. *Measurement and observation.* Skill in making observations is of fundamental importance: watch for instrument errors, repeat observations and acquire a reasonable range of observations, recording them in a neat and organised manner.

4. *Handling data.* Assess the reliability of your conclusions: estimate the source and size of errors in observing and processing data. Critically appraise your work: identify where something went wrong or could have been done better.

Chapter 10

The GNVQ Portfolio

Your GNVQ portfolio is a collection of your GNVQ work. It is the main proof that you have fulfilled the requirements of a GNVQ.

10.1 What goes into it

Be aware of the wide *range* of material that can go into your portfolio. Such awareness will help you to do the work, and make the work more interesting and more successful.

Much will be *paper-based prose*: reports on projects, essays, notes, logs, schedules for activities, questionnaires, comments from your assessor or from those who have seen you in action on work experience, and write-ups on your contribution to group work.

There will also be *visual and audio* material: diagrams, graphs, photographs, sketch maps or video; and recorded discussions, interviews, presentations and assessor commentary.

Then there are things that you may have *made*: models, sculpture, and art or design work in two and three dimensions.

A portfolio can thus be more than an A4 file. It may involve boxes, or large containers for art work. You must therefore *organise* your portfolio carefully, right from the start. It should be easily understandable to an outsider. You will help yourself if you write it up as you go along.

You must keep a careful *record* of everything you do, even of such things as teacher help. Your GNVQ at Distinction level is as much about the process of learning as about the level that your work achieves, so beware omitting to record what you do because you feel it's not relevant. Recording also covers relating your assignment to the relevant unit or units (remember that an assignment can go towards satisfying parts of more than one unit).

The *core skills* of IT, Number and Communication are covered while you compile your portfolio, and are not bolted on as an extra. Consult subject specialists at the point when you need help in these areas. In the case of IT, you can also ask some knowledgeable friends, write down the points, and have them near your computer.

It is difficult to overemphasise the importance of *work experience* to your GNVQ. GNVQs are about being in touch with modern commercial and industrial practices; consequently any links that you can get with industry will raise the level of your work. Ideally you need a range of contacts, for single days or longer. Work experience requires planning, and depends on the goodwill of the local community. Be ever-conscious of this: hence you need a good letter of enquiry and a thank-you note afterwards.

There is no set *amount* of work that you must have in your portfolio, and earlier work can be replaced by later work. The key is to cover the requirements of the unit specifications, or syllabus. It follows that you have to be fully familiar with the specifications.

10.2 How to create it

Creating a good portfolio begins with understanding the requirements as detailed in the GNVQ literature. Some of the language may at first seem remote and unfamiliar.

1. *Understanding your GNVQ.* The syllabus (subject specifications) of your GNVQ is divided into parts (units). Each part consists of activities (elements) on which you will be assessed. For each activity there is a means of judging if you have done the activity successfully (performance criteria), and there are details of the extent and depth of the coverage required (range statements) and information about the approach needed (evidence indicators).

The subject specifications of a GNVQ

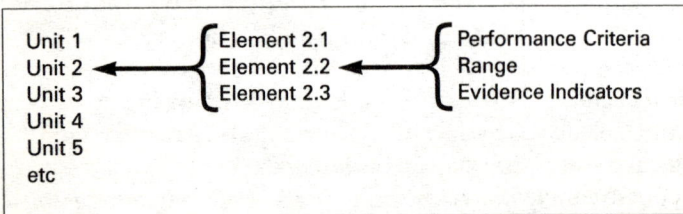

98

2. *Translating its words into action.* The above is the order in which these terms appear in a GNVQ publication. This is how to translate them into what you have to do:

Step 1:	look at the element: this is your *title*
Step 2:	look at the evidence indicators: these are your *instructions*
Step 3:	look at the range: this *sets limits* on your coverage
Step 4:	look at the performance criteria: these tell you what to *do*. Turn them from passive to active (eg, 'A marketing plan is identified' becomes 'Identify a marketing plan')

10.3 Conducting surveys

Survey work is important in GNVQs. It is part of the core skill Number, and will come into GNVQs such as Advanced Business (eg a survey of the leisure interests of a group of business-women).

Here are some pointers:

Step 1. Purpose

You must be clear on your exact purpose. Only then can you devise appropriate questions.

Step 2. Questions

The key to running a questionnaire successfully is: work out how you will analyse your responses when you work out your questions. At the end of this section on pp 101–105 are some models to follow. You will see that the questions are 'closed-ended'. Open-ended questions, where the subject is allowed to write a free response, can provide insightful data, but are much harder to analyse; in these cases, you would select representative quotations for your write-up.

Questions should:

(a) be clear
(b) have only one possible meaning
(c) use simple language

(d) omit vague words

(e) avoid two negative words

(f) not contain 'if'.

Step 3. Layout of questionnaire

This is vital to its success. The questionnaire should:

(a) be typed

(b) start with a pleasant introductory paragraph to arouse interest and gain co-operation

(c) say what the information is for, and assure confidentiality
and anonymity

(d) order the questions carefully, with very simple ones first

(e) leave space between questions to help the reader (and you)

(f) lay out the response areas horizontally across the page or on
the right hand side, for easier analysis

(g) give a relatively early return date.

Step 4. Pilot the questionnaire

Try it out on people similar to those for whom it is intended.
Piloting reveals weaknesses so that you can correct them.

Step 5. Work out your sample

If you are forced to use people from your target group who are
available at the time and willing (an opportunity sample), do so,
but indicate this clearly in your write-up, and bear in mind that
you cannot generalise your results as confidently. You really need
a representative sample (eg, every tenth person on an alphabetical list of 100). Choose the first one by putting a pin in the list. If
the tenth one won't do it, use the eleventh.

Step 6. Sources of error

When interpreting your results, consider possible sources of
error. They may very well not apply; the point is to consider the
possibility:

(a) social acceptability, where people choose the socially acceptable answer

(b) response set, where a person tends to either agree or disagree with questions

(c) bias towards the centre, where a person always goes for the middle response.

Five sample questions as models with how to analyse them

Example 1

A *Yes/No* item can be analysed by using a percentage

Do you think that the position of women has improved over the past 10 years?

Yes ☐

No ☐

Level of agreement that the position of women has improved over the last 10 years:

Number of yes responses:	$20/80 \times 100 = 25\%$
Number of no responses:	$60/80 \times 100 = 75\%$

Note: $n = 80$

Example 2

An Attitude item can be analysed by using a bar chart

Britain is pulling out of its economic troubles.
Please circle the number which corresponds with your answer.

strongly disagree	disagree	neutral	agree	strongly agree
1	2	3	4	5

Level of agreement that Britain is pulling out of its economic troubles:

strongly disagree	disagree	neutral	agree	strongly agree
15	35	25	15	10

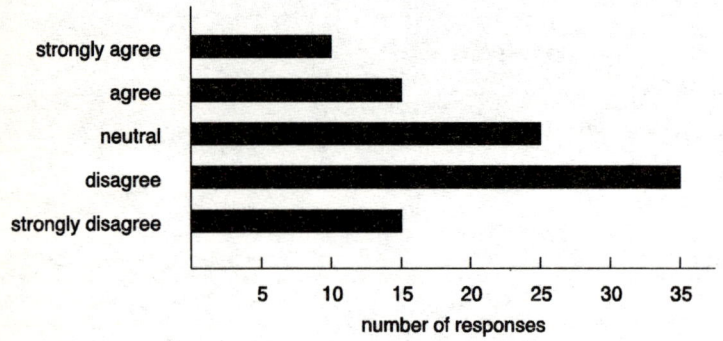

Note 1: n = 100
Note 2: the number of responses for each category has been added up
Note 3: the bars are all 4mm wide.

Example 3

Rank order items can be analysed by working out a rank order number.

Rank the following leisure activities in your order of preference.

In the boxes below,
first put 1 for the most preferred
then put 2 for the next preferred
then put 3 for the least preferred

seeing friends ☐
watching television ☐
reading books ☐

Rank order of preference, three leisure pursuits

Category	Responses of 10 students										Total	Rank
Seeing friends	1	1	3	1	3	1	1	1	1	1	14	1
Watching television	3	3	2	3	2	3	2	3	3	2	26	3
Reading books	2	2	1	2	1	2	3	2	2	3	20	2

Note 1: the lowest total ranks one.
Note 2: n = 10

Example 4

For *Grouped data*, use a histogram

How many staff does your organisation employ?

0–49   50–99   100–149   150–199

<u>Number of staff employed by organisations represented in survey</u>

staff	number of firms
0–49	10
50–99	30
100–149	50
150–199	10

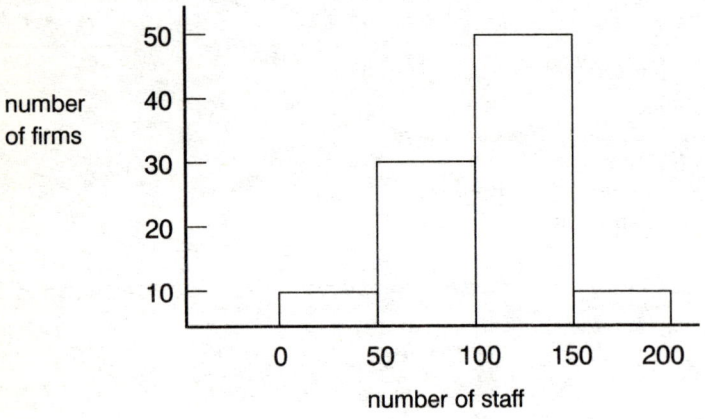

Note 1: add the number of responses for each category
Note 2: the bars are touching and of equal width.

Example 5

Semantic Differential forms of response

The Advanced GNVQ in Health and Social Care requires knowledge of 'semantic differential' forms of response. These can be useful, as they are readily understood and easy to write. Examples are given below. You circle the number that corresponds with your answer. They are analysed like Example 2 of the models on p. 102.

Prime Minister	weak	1 2 3 4 5 6 7	strong
Leisure Provision	bad	1 2 3 4 5 6 7	good
Health Education	ineffective	1 2 3 4 5 6 7	effective

For the first example (Prime Minister), put the word 'strong' at the top of the vertical axis. Underneath it put the numbers 7 down to 1, then the word 'weak'. The horizontal axis would show the total number of responses for each category. The other two items (Leisure Provision, Health Education) would each have their own bar chart.

Chapter 11

The Psychology of Study

The ideas and content of this book are presented in such a way that you can use them, but they are underpinned by a psychological base. It is interesting to examine this base separately, as it will further reinforce what has been said.

11.1 Motivation

1. *Goal setting*. People exert themselves more when a target has been set. The target must be realistic, though. Thus, when you sit down to work, you should have a target amount that you wish to complete in a given time, preferably a complete unit of work. You therefore feel a *compulsion* to finish it, and a sense of *achievement* when you have done so. You need a specific and clearly defined objective.
2. *Abolishing procrastination rituals*. It can be very difficult to start a task. This is often a problem with painters who are unable to start work on a blank canvas. 'Jump into the water' by starting punctually at the allotted time.
3. *Concentration* is intense attention. You have to 'park' your mind on the task by trying to pick out the important *details*. The greater your concentration, the more effective your learning.
4. *Competition*. This can be a motivator. Co-operation can be a bigger one. Discussion with a fellow student or mutual testing can be a big bonus. More use could be made of collaborative learning. Work out between you other ways in which it can be done. However, both of you must know the material quite well to collaborate really fruitfully.
5. *Modelling*. It can help to model yourself on good students.

For example, when do good students start to revise (this was discussed on p. 70); what sort of revision notes do they make? Think carefully about what the really good students in your group do.

6. *Habit.* Effectiveness in any sphere requires habit. It is an *automatic* response as a result of repetition; for this reason, it is a powerful force to have on your side, eg work from 7 to 9 pm each weekday evening; or always jot down ideas for an essay at the moment they come into your head. You need to exercise judgement, though: unreflective habit can also constrain learning, eg habitually reading in one way, unaware of scanning or skimming.

7. *Interest* is a strong motivator. You can increase your interest by *having views* on what you are studying. You then become emotionally involved in your work. Also, as far as possible, choose books which put points in an interesting way. If you don't like one book, have the confidence to reject it and find another.

8. *Self-questioning.* The constant posing of questions to yourself generates activity. By simply asking yourself questions, you feel urged to find the answers: 'How does this work?'; 'What does this word mean?'; 'Why was this policy adopted?' You can sense a pull to action.

9. *Self-concept.* Try to work out in your mind a picture of the sort of person you want to be. You'll then tend to become that.

11.2 Thinking

There are four main types of thinking:

1. *Logical thinking*, which means reasoning. In its narrow sense it involves drawing conclusions from facts, as in Mathematics. More widely, it involves activities such as arriving at a general statement on the basis of particular instances, and trying to prove or disprove arguments, as in arts subjects.

2. *Creative thinking* means perceiving new relationships between facts and ideas. This comes into essay writing, for example. Its stages are:

   (a) Preparation: you gather your material.
   (b) Incubation: you let the material and the question simmer in the unconscious (hence the need to start essays early).

    (c) Illumination: you allow ideas to emerge into conscious-
ness.

    (d) Elaboration: you communicate your ideas on paper.

    (e) Evaluation: you check over what you have written to see
whether it says what you intended it to say. You criticise,
modify and improve.

3.   *Lateral thinking* is a type of creative thinking identified by
Edward de Bono. Problems are solved by rejecting the ordinary way of looking at them, and choosing an entirely different way. Here is an example: it is a trick from a trick shop
which requires lateral thinking in order to find a solution.
You have to get both balls into the cupped shelves at each
end of the container.

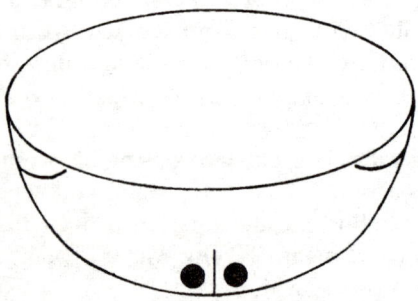

The ordinary way of trying to do this would be to tilt the
plastic container – but as you try to get the second ball in, the
first one falls out! The lateral thinking solution is to spin the
container, so that both balls go into their holes simultane-
ously by centrifugal force.

4.   *Intuitive thinking*. This is where a small amount of information is given and you make an intuitive leap to a solution.

11.3 Memory

With attention, material passes into short-term memory (STM).
This is a type of echo box. STM holds material for up to 30 sec-
onds, remembering it by sound, eg a telephone number which
you have looked up can be remembered by repeating it (which is
what people do). STM can remember about seven items, and is
easily disrupted: for instance, the telephone number will slip out

of your mind if someone disturbs you, though if you are not disturbed, the retrieval of the information is error-free. However, STM cannot improve its performance above about seven items, although 'chunking' helps, as when the telephone operator gives you the number in pairs or chunks, as follows:

four figure number 24/68
five figure number 24/685
six figure number 24/68/57

Long-term memory (LTM) is different. It is a type of filing cabinet. It can hold material from minutes to decades, and it remembers by analysis. Its capacity is unlimited and it is less easily disrupted than STM, though retrieval is more error-prone. It can, however, improve, as follows.

Material is transferred from STM to LTM by thinking about it, repeating it and using it. This transfer is achieved by: analysing; understanding; discussion; exercises; answering past questions; self-testing; making diagrams; and compiling revision notes.

Retrieval from LTM is best accomplished by putting questions to yourself. Searching then takes place and recall develops by free association (ie, letting one idea lead to another). Free association is an important technique in tackling exam essays. Here is an example:

Free association to recall the name of a student who left four years ago.

She had brown eyes.
She was tall.
She played hockey.
She was friends with Wendy.
She told good jokes.
She became a dentist.
Her name was *Sophie*.

Key words in revision notes act as cues to help retrieval.

Forgetting is a real threat, and happens because of retroactive inhibition (ie, later knowledge buries earlier knowledge), and because of fading, though more the former than the latter. Poor concentration, poor understanding and high anxiety also contribute.

The keys to a good memory are understanding knowledge, organising it into a meaningful structure, and going over it repeatedly, alternating looking at it with trying to recall what's there.

11.4 Approaches to learning

There are two main approaches to learning:

1. *Rote learning*. This is learning by heart, or learning 'parrot fashion'. It has a place in advanced work (eg, in learning quotations for English) but its place is limited, because advanced work is not simply the reproduction of knowledge.
2. *Learning by understanding*. This is the key learning approach to all advanced work. It is the central aim of your effort.

11.5 Ways of learning

Some key learning principles are:

1. *Activity*. Learning is an active process. Do not passively sit and read notes and books: *actively* try to recall what is there; think about past questions; organise material. Have opinions in class, and state them.
2. *Organisation of material*. Gestalt psychologists believe that the mind actively tries to organise what is experienced into a meaningful pattern, or construction. Parts which do not seem to fit may be discarded.

   Good students assist the mind's attempts to structure knowledge by structuring it themselves, trying to fit details into a wider whole. Hence, for an essay, read something short first to gain an overview. Before reading a chapter of a detailed book, it is a good idea to try to appraise the chapter as a whole by looking over the headings and subheadings. When making a revision note, try to put a whole topic (or a whole aspect of a topic) on one side.

   When learning something, it should first be read through entirely to get the general drift. Then break it down into as small 'wholes' as possible in order to achieve errorless learning. Learn them by repeating them and trying to recall them, perfecting one at a time. Repetitions should alternate with acts of recall. It is safest to look immediately when you cannot remember, to avoid implanting guesses in your mind. Repetition usually takes the form of reading over the material.

3. *Spaced repetition.* Periods of repetition-and-recall should be relatively brief (perhaps 15 minutes), and well distributed. The intervals give the material time to sink in. Hence, start memory work early for tests, instead of concentrating into one sitting all the time that can be given to the particular task. If you end up having only one evening, try to repeat-and-recall periodically between 7 and 9 pm.

4. *Retroactive inhibition.* This is interference with the memory of one set of material caused by the learning of another set: later learning covers up earlier memories. Learning before you go to bed, say at the end of your 7 to 9 pm study period, is a good idea so long as you are not too tired, because retroactive inhibition is avoided. Learning before you go to bed is advantageous because there is a lack of later learning, as sleep follows, though it will inhibit learning which has taken place earlier in the day. Perhaps it is best done as a review of the day's work. Learning deep into the night is different though, and not a good idea: attention fades, and fatigue follows the next day.

5. *Review.* One calls this revision. There are three types:

    (a) *Immediate revision* (review just after you have been taught the material)
    (b) *Maintenance revision* (review between learning and testing for the final time)
    (c) *Terminal revision* (review just before final testing).

    All are important. Their order of effectiveness is: terminal, immediate, maintenance.

    Repetition of material during each of the three types of review is important, as repetition is a vital learning principle.

6. *Overlearning.* Forgetting is an enormous problem. Details slip away very quickly. So long as you can understand the material initially, details can be brushed up by revision notes, but the rapidity of forgetting is one reason why revision for A Levels is so much emphasised in this book. It is important to *overlearn*. Overlearning means the continued revision of material even when it seems to be known perfectly, eg going over revision notes again and again. Overlearning is a protection against forgetfulness caused by anxiety in the exam room.

7. *Recency.* The best remembered items are those most recently experienced. Hence, revision notes should be gone over right up to the last minute before the exam. Being short, they are an ideal way of using the principle of recency.

8. *Knowledge of results.* You can use the principle on yourself by assessing how you are getting on in achieving the work target of each session. Tell yourself 'how you are doing'. You may say to yourself: 'I must work more quickly to meet my target', or 'I'm doing well tonight – I must keep it up.' Check that you remember each small chunk of work before you go on to the next one.

9. *Reinforcement.* When you perform an act of desired behaviour, you reinforce it by rewarding yourself. You will recognise this concept at work in the comments on pp 76–77 on the use of time during the Christmas holiday of the second year of A Levels, and you'll probably remember receiving 'merit marks' as a child, at primary school. The reinforcement should come immediately after the desired behaviour, eg having a coffee straight after completing a unit of work. The concept is used more loosely in the discussion on how to increase mid-course A Level motivation on p 74.

11.6 The SQ3R method

One method of reading and note making, which was created to combine all the important psychological principles of study, is the SQ3R method of F P Robinson, from Ohio State University. It has found its way into many study books in a diluted form. It is given here briefly but in its original form.

1. *Survey.* One minute. Look at the headings and final summary of the chapter.

2. *Question.* Turn the first heading into a question.

3. *Read.* Read the whole section to find the answer to the question.

4. *Recite.* Compile 'working notes' as follows:

    (a) work from memory, but peek if you have to
    (b) write down the heading
    (c) note key words and phrases, with examples
    (d) use your own words where possible
    (e) be brief.

Stages two, three and four are repeated with all the remaining sections of the chapter.

5. *Review*. Five minutes. Look at the overall layout of your note and then test yourself by covering up points, recalling and checking.

This method is very effective for mastering a textbook, but you cannot combine material from different books into one note. Robinson's work is stimulating, and can be followed up in: Robinson, F P (1970) *Effective Study*, New York: Harper & Row.

Chapter 12

Techniques of Mental Management

In order to study really effectively, you have to feel good about yourself. This means feeling that you are in control of your own life. There are some techniques that can help you.

12.1 Present moment living

Our lives are made up of a series of present moments joined together. You can never be physically present in any place at any particular moment other than the place you are in. But one part of you can be somewhere else: your thoughts.

This is a problem for many people. They allow negative or destructive thoughts to intrude. These may be guilt about the past, or worry about the future. Their present moments are therefore sabotaged.

What you can do about it is this:

1. *The past*. As far is the past is concerned, you have to *learn* from it. You may now know how you could have done better, but you didn't have that insight then. You cannot return to the past and re-do it; so instead, learn from it. It follows that you must *forgive yourself* for your shortcomings. You did the best you could with what you knew then. You must also *forgive others*. In forgiving others, you do not need to like them or respect them, only forgive them, or resentment could ruin you.

2. *The future*. As for the future, *act now*, in the present, so as to work towards certain future *outcomes* (or goals).

3. *The present*. You will now be living much more in the present.

You need to function well in the present, in the 'here and now', to feel good. In each present moment of your life, you need to do the right thing in the right way. Focus on making the present as fulfilling as possible.

These ideas can be followed up in Deyer W (1976) *Your Erroneous Zones*, London: Sphere.

12.2 Relaxation technique

Here is an instant calming sequence.

1. *Breathing.* Slow down your breathing, taking longer with the breathing out than the breathing in, ie make the breath out like a relaxing sigh.
2. *Smile.* Just smile to yourself. It relaxes the muscles of your face and makes you feel better.
3. *Posture.* Have a balanced posture, feeling as if suspended gently from a hook in the top of your head.
4. *Relaxation of muscles.* Imagine you are standing in a hot shower, and as the water washes over you, it washes all the muscle tension and joint stiffness away down the drainage hole of the shower.
5. *Thought control.* Day-dream for a moment, and let your mind go to a favourite Happy Place, or imagine you are on the beach of a tropical island. Get in touch with all your feelings there. When you are very relaxed press your left elbow with the fingers of your right hand and return your thoughts to the present. Keep on practising the above, and you will soon find that just pressing yourself on the left elbow will make you feel emotionally and physically relaxed.

12.3 Pre-enforcement of future success

This is an extension of the above technique. Instead of visualising a Happy Place, you visualise yourself being relaxed in the exam, or doing practical work or answering oral questions effectively.

You are more likely to do these things successfully in reality because you have already done them successfully in your mind: you have in effect done them once already. This technique works because the unconscious mind cannot tell the difference between reality and things you have only vividly imagined.

12.4 Sleep

It is a big disadvantage to have less sleep than you personally need. I can recall a potential grade A student ending up with a grade E through lack of sleep. I walked up and down beside her in the exam room to keep her awake! If you do not get the amount of sleep that you personally need, your cerebral activity goes down, and errors and mis-perceptions increase. You also become more irritable and more prone to illness.

So how much sleep do people need? A small number need less than 5 hours or over ten hours. Everyone else is in between. Girls need more sleep than boys, and people need more sleep at 16 than at 18. When stressed or ill, even with a cold, you need more sleep, than when physically and emotionally fit. An appropriate generalisation would be eight hours' sleep, from 11 pm to 7 am.

But the crucial principle is: you should ascertain by experience the amount of sleep you need to feel really good, then make sure you get it. If you are constantly having to be woken up by the alarm clock, you are not getting enough sleep for you.

12.5 Anxiety

You may find Collier's Formula helpful. The original form dates from the eighteenth century.

Take a sheet of paper and divide it horizontally down the middle. Complete the left-hand column first, then the right-hand one.

Left column	*Right column*
What is the worst thing that could happen over this?	Having come to terms with it:
Then whatever that worst thing is – accept it in your mind, and come to terms with it.	What can I do to prevent the worst happening? Act immediately.

12.6 Depression

A problem-solving approach can help, if you aren't too depressed. Try to think ideally what you want: in what way do you want your situation to be different? Talking to someone who will listen, care and understand, will help. Then form a plan to achieve what you want. You may be able to alter your environment in your favour, or alternatively to see things differently.

Your depression may be more serious, in which case you should see your GP. If you are becoming withdrawn, losing your joy of life, or have had a significant life event such as a bereavement, your parents recently being divorced or a parent being made redundant, your treatment can include anti-depressant medication to change the brain chemistry back to normal. These medicines are not tranquillisers and they are not addictive.

12.7 Stress

There is a flow chart, on the following page, showing how to take the anguish out of stress, which then becomes useful pressure. The value of exercise cannot be over-stated. It helps to counteract stress, anxiety and both mild and severe depression. There are physiological benefits and also cognitive benefits, in that it makes you feel more vital. Ten to fifteen minutes each day is enough to have an effect, or 20–30 minutes three times a week. Vigorous exercise is needed; lower levels are less effective. A brisk walk would be OK.

Managing stress

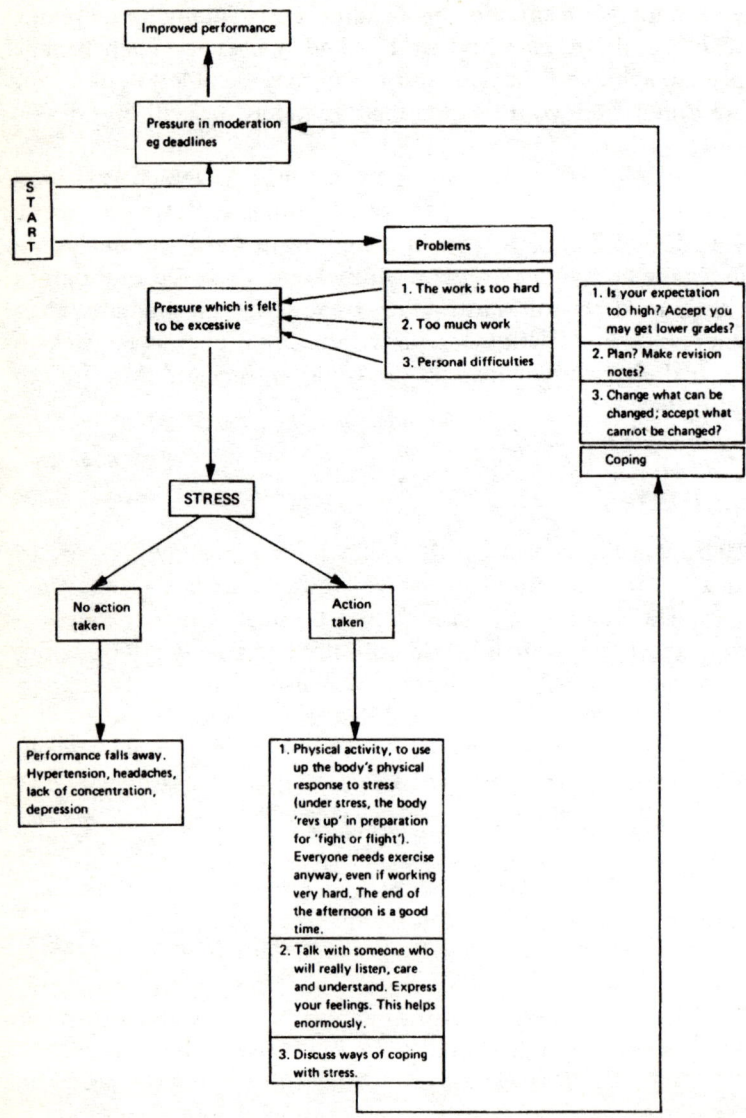

Chapter 13

Revision Notes

It is now time to look at how the concept of structure can help with the consolidation of knowledge, and this brings us to consider revision notes, or summary notes, ie brief outlines of the material to be remembered.

13.1 Making revision notes

There are three key points to remember when making revision notes:

1. The *structure* of the revision note should be crystal clear. The outline should stand out clearly so that the development of the revision note strikes home as you look at it. The headings of the note should develop logically. A revision note can be compared with seeing a person through an X-ray. The skeleton is apparent and 'hangs together' as your eyes move downwards from head to toe.
2. *Large (A4) sheets of paper* are used. More can be contained on them and the structure of material more easily grasped. The paper can be unlined or have narrow lines. Going back to the skeleton image, one wants the whole skeleton on one piece of paper. Ideally, a whole topic (or a whole aspect of a topic) should have a side all to itself. Condensation of material on to a few sheets of paper is a large boost to confidence, for you no longer feel swamped by the quantity of material to be learned.
3. The revision note should contain some well chosen *landmark words*. These are key words which hint at the details to be remembered, and act as triggers or cues to areas of details within the overall structure. In the skeleton image, they would correspond to the key organs of the body.

Revision notes can be made throughout your course. You can make them for mid-course tests and these will probably be thrown away after they have served their purpose.

Nearer the end of your course, you will make your final revision notes. At this point your understanding of the material will have deepened, and you will be able to 'stand back' from it more easily. Revision notes made now will include only the very best material. They will be carefully organised. Having thought about them so much, you will virtually know the material on their completion, but you must then go for absolute mastery. You must *over*learn them.

A revision note can be mastered as follows. First look over the revision note as a whole, then break it down into as small 'wholes' or 'cells' as possible. Go over a 'cell', then try to recall it. You will have to recall it in the exam room, and it is as well to practise. When you cannot recall a point, it is safest to look straight away to avoid sowing guesses in your mind. Repeat and recall alternately. Master each small chunk before you go on to the next one but stick to short memory sessions, having many of them. When you have mastered each revision note in turn in this way, return to the first one and start all over again. Continue to learn them by this method even when you know them perfectly. Overlearning will help you to recall them under the pressure of the exam room.

There is no such thing as a model revision note. Any revision note is a model if it is felt to be of use by its maker. Some people prefer a spaced out, to a cluttered, format.

Here is a revision note on War Art. The main note appears first, followed by the revision note made from it.

WAR ART

Introduction

1. The film conveys continuing reality, and therefore has immediacy.
2. The photograph captures the split-second happening and emphasises seeing.
3. War art conveys feeling.

War art conveys feeling

1. Moore. He liked reclining figures. He portrayed people lying down in the tube during bombing. He conveys their feeling of weariness.

The people and place fuse together to create the feeling of claustrophobia.

2. <u>Searle</u>. He drew the horrors of building a railway in the Far East. He conveys the feeling of barbarity.

War art uses symbolism

1. <u>Nash</u>. The devastated landscape in 'Menin Road' symbolises a generation devastated by war. He combines realism and surrealism.
2. Spencer. He painted a picture of a pile of crosses, intermingled with soldiers and pack animals rising from the dead. Christ is the central figure in the heap. The crosses are a symbol. They are mass produced, thus a symbol of impersonality; and they are a symbol of hope of an after-life.

War art shows awareness of line

1. <u>Nevinson's</u> machine gunners painting uses straight lines and sharp angles to convey brutality. The gunners are dehumanised by the gun, hinting at the dehumanising effect of machine warfare. His control accentuates the terror.
2. <u>Wyndham Lewis's</u> 'A Battery Shelled'. The officers are detached and remote (curved lines); the men are tense under fire (angular lines).

War art can depict the less obvious sides of war

1. <u>Ardizzone</u>. He depicts humour: the Home Guard frisk an Englishman.
2. <u>Sutherland</u>. His 'Fallen Lift Shaft' notes beauty in destruction.

Revision note

<u>WAR ART</u>

Film of photograph of war art.

<u>Feeling</u>	— Moore	(figures)	Searle	(railway)
<u>Symbolism</u>	— Nash	(landscape)	Spencer	(crosses)
<u>Line</u>	— Nevinson	(gunners)	Lewis	(battery)
<u>Unobvious</u>	— Ardizzone	(frisking)	Sutherland	(beauty)

13.2 Variations on revision notes

There are three possible variations:

1. *Overmarking*. Some people like to mark over main headings and key points in their ordinary notes, using a special over-marking pen. This is useful if the structure is not clear.

2. *Margin notation.* Headings and key words can be written in the margin or ordinary notes. Again, this clarifies the structure if that is necessary.
3. *Index cards.* These can be used for revision notes instead of sheets of A4 paper.

Their underlying principles are the same as for a standard revision note and if they work for you, use them.

13.3 Personal choice in revision notes

Some examples will help you to develop your own style of revision note.

Example 1: for Advanced GNVQ in Business

The example, shown on p 123, condenses one unit of the course on to one side. This is a very good revision note, with some interesting features. The left-hand third of the page consists of words which you could look at, while covering up and trying to recall what is on the right. The right-hand side uses two columns. Key names are in boxes. There is a lot here, but it doesn't seem overloaded as there is good use of space. If in doubt, write less rather than more. This revision note is not the result of a single draft; a revision note is an artistic creation. Doing it more than once helps to create a better result, and the process of creating helps you to learn the material.

Example 2: for A Level History

An index card made as part of revision for History A Level is shown on p 124. For me, the material is not well structured: points are noted from different writers, but similar points should have been grouped together under headings. And inevitably with index cards, large areas of material cannot be taken in at a glance. Nevertheless the student found it helpful, which is what counts.

Example 3: for A Level Pure Maths

Page 125 shows one side of a nine-sided note for Pure Maths A Level, written by a student who went on to read Business Studies at university. It is clear and concise. An interesting point is the use of the split page, working down one column at a time. This is very suitable for Maths.

Revision note for Advanced GNVQ in Business

ATTITUDES AND PERFORMANCE AT WORK

Attitudes created by.....

	Content	Context
1. Job		
2. Management	W functional	W participative
3. Needs met	MASLOW	hierarchy
4. Culture	power	− submit
	status	− compete
	task	− autonomy
	person	− serves p
5. Inter-dept	MINTZBERG	
	strategic apex	support structure
	middle line	
	operating core	technostructure

Motivation affected by....

1. Internal "energise"	ALDERFER (ERG)	McCLELLAND (need)	
	existence	N − Ach	
	relatedness	N − Aff	
	growth	N − Power	
2. Social "channel"	VROOM (exp)	ADAMS (equ)	
	$M = P \times V$	input = output	
3. (Dis)satisfiers "sustain"	HERZBERG		
	satisfiers in job itself	dissatisfiers in environ	
	achievement	working condits	
	recognition	relationships	
	responsibility	salary piece	
		basic + bon	
		perf rel	

Monitoring

1. Appraisal	feedback	
	motivation	
	promotion	
2. Job redesign	job enrichment	job rotation

Example 4: for A Level English Literature

Pages 126 and 127 show the second half of a revision note on Dylan Thomas written by an A Level English Literature student who went on to read English at university. It deals with 'poetry and words', 'convention' and 'method' (the first half, which is of similar length, deals with 'birth', 'fruitfulness' and 'death'). The headings and subheadings are clear, and the student found it very helpful. It represents good condensation. My own inclination would be to try to condense it even more, and to structure the material within subheadings in a more visually appealing way. I do not feel this strongly, though, and I would rate this a very solid revision note. The main point is that it helped the student.

Index card revision note for A Level History (see p 122)

EDWARD VI 1547–1553

1) Elton : 'a cold-hearted prig' & his reign as full of
'disastrous policies & insensitive politicians'; the reduction of
'the king-worship of the early 16th to absurdity.'

2.) Hoskyns & Morris. could have turned out to be the most
dazzling Tudor king.

3.) Morris : the reign 'tested the constitutional empire
constructed by H. VIII & T. Cromwell, & proved that
it could survive recklessness during & could ever
survive being put into reverse.'

4.) Morris : 'S might have done much for Eng.,
whereas Dudley brought her very near to ruin.'

5.) Paget : 'Commons is become a king; a king
appointing conditions & laws to the governors.'

Revision note for A Level Pure Maths (see p 122)

(see p 122)

Partial Fractions

1. $\dfrac{x}{(x+1)(x+3)}$ can be split

   $\dfrac{x^2}{(x+1)(x+3)}$ divide 1st

2. $\dfrac{x}{(x+1)(x+3)} \equiv \dfrac{A}{x+1} + \dfrac{B}{x+3}$

3. $\dfrac{2x^2-3}{(x-1)^3(x+1)} \equiv \dfrac{A}{x-1} + \dfrac{B}{(x-1)^2} + \dfrac{C}{(x-1)^3} + \dfrac{D}{x+1}$

4. $\dfrac{x+1}{(x-1)(x^2+1)} \equiv \dfrac{A}{x-1} + \dfrac{Bx+C}{x^2+1}$ N.B. Common denominator

Use of P.F.

1. Eg. expanding functions in ascending powers of x.

Work out P.F. to e.g. $\dfrac{1}{1-x} + \dfrac{x-1}{1+x^2}$

Binomial T. using $(1-x)^{-1} + (x-1)(1+x^2)^{-1}$

2. Integration.

Summation of Series

1. A.P. e.g. $1+2+3+4+r \ldots +n$

   $a=1 \quad d=1 \quad n=n$

   $S_n = \dfrac{n}{2}(2 + (n-1)d)$

   $\sum_{r=1}^{n} r = \dfrac{n}{2}(n+1)$

   $\sum_{r=1}^{n} r^2 = \dfrac{n}{6}(n+1)(2n+1)$

   $\sum_{r=1}^{n} r^3 = \dfrac{n^2}{4}(n+1)^2$

Integration by Substitution

1. $\int (1+2x)^{10}\, dx \quad u = 1+2x$

2. $\int \sqrt{4-x^2}\, dx \quad x = 2\sin\theta$ i.e. $2\sin\theta$ (a^2)

   $\dfrac{dx}{d\theta} = 2\cos\theta$

   $dx = 2\cos\theta\, d\theta$

$\int \sqrt{4-4\sin^2\theta}\, dx$

$\int 2\sqrt{1-\sin^2\theta}\; 2\cos\theta\, d\theta$

$\int 2\cos\theta \times 2\cos\theta\, d\theta$

$\int 4\cos^2\theta\, d\theta$

3. Odd powers of $\sin x \cdot \cos x$

   $u = \cos x$ for o.p. of $\sin x$

   $u = \sin x$ for o.p. of $\cos x$

   $\therefore \int \sin^5 x\, dx \qquad u = \cos x$

   $\int \sin^5 x\, \dfrac{du}{-\sin x} \qquad \dfrac{du}{dx} = -\sin x$

   $\int -\sin^4 x\, du$

   $\int -\sin^2 x\, \sin^2 x\, du$

   $= \int (1-\cos^2 x)(1-\cos^2 x)\, du$

   $= \int (1-u^2)(1-u^2)\, du$

4. e.g. $\int \dfrac{dx}{a+b\cos x}$ or $\int \dfrac{dx}{a+b\sin x}$

   $\cos x = \dfrac{1-t^2}{1+t^2}$

   $t = \tan\dfrac{x}{2}$

   $\dfrac{dt}{dx} = \dfrac{1}{2}\sec^2\dfrac{x}{2}$

   $= \dfrac{1}{2}\left[1 + \tan^2\dfrac{x}{2}\right]$

   $= \dfrac{1}{2}[1+t^2]$

   $dx = \dfrac{2\,dt}{1+t^2}$

   $\therefore \int \dfrac{dx}{2+\cos x} = \int \dfrac{2\,dt}{1+t^2} \times \dfrac{1}{\left[2 + \frac{1-t^2}{1+t^2}\right]}$

   $\int \dfrac{2\,dt}{3+t^2}$ Standard form

Integration by Parts

$uv - \int v \cdot \dfrac{du}{dx}\, dx$

1. $\int \log x \cdot dx \qquad u = \log x \quad \dfrac{dv}{dx} = 1$

   $\dfrac{du}{dx} = \dfrac{1}{x} \qquad v = x$

   $x\log x - \int 1\, dx \qquad \log x$ must $= u$ because

   $= x\log x - x + c \qquad$ it can't be integrated as v

2) Type of product involving using parts twice

   eg $\int x^2 \cdot \sin x\, dx$

   eg $\int e^x \sin x\, dx = -e^x \cos x + \int e^x \cos x\, dx$

   $= -e^x \cos x + e^x \sin x - \int e^x \sin x\, dx$

   $2\int e^x \sin x = -e^x \cos x + e^x \sin x$

   $\int e^x \sin x = \dfrac{-e^x \cos x}{2} + \dfrac{e^x \sin x}{2}$

Revision note for A Level English Literature (see p 124)

POETRY + WORDS

① "Especially when the October wind"
- Tyranny of words. "My busy heart who shudders as she talks
  Sheds the syllabic blood and drains her words"
- dependence on "heartless words"
- should put new value on "neural meaning" deeper level.
- listen to the message of the "dark vowelled birds"
- to prevent words taking over + "the coming fury of second comings
  centre constructs"

- Mind has caused 'crabbing sea' 'a raven cough'
  "frosty fingers punish the land"
- end of language
  "Shut in a tower of words" (Ivory tower - detached)

② "The hand that signed the paper."
- hands that write have so much power.
  "Hands have no tears to flow"

③ "Once it was the colour of saying"
- desire for new poetry
- yet "And every stone I laid of like a real" (stone-hard,
  no feeling.)

④ "Hunchback in the Park"
- desire for perfection "A woman figure without fault
  straight as a young elm"

⑤ "La Danseuse"
- the dancer so perfect "Her form was like a poet's mind"

⑥ "Light Breaks where no sun shines"
- new consciousness, deeper
  "Dawn breaks behind the eyes"

Auden "All I have is a voice"

⑦ "Time held me green + dying/Though I sang in my chains like the sea"
  · Fern Hill
  of words

CONVENTION

① "I see the Boys of Summer"
- Boys, destroy harvest, freeze seeds in soil, mind in love, decay
  sweetness of summer with thoughts of Summer
  "I see the poles of summer in the ice"
  "Of frozen loves they fetch their girls"
  "There in the sun the mad tidbits
  of doubt and dark they'd other nerves"

- with to oppose all, draw opposite out of everything
  "But seasons must be challenged" · Apostles
- convention of love + sex "A muscling up from lovers in their strange position"
  "Here love's damp muscle dries + dies"
- reversal · Spring → Christmas "In Spring across our foreheads with holly"
  · earth "Hold up the noisy sea + drop their birds."

⑤ "After the Funeral"
- convention of rel. "hie with religion in their cramp" c/f "I see
- remove routine from life ... until
  The stuffed lung of the fox twitch & dry cry here
  And the strutting fern lays seeds on the
    black sill' (hanging)
- convention must break down
  "break down the walls of the fenced dry wood"

Fern Hill "Now as I was young & easy under the apple boughs
  About the cuttey house & happy as the grass was green"
sound creates
sense

METHOD ① Struggle of "stripping away darkness & struggling up to light"
       ② Feeling rather than thought. Not an intellectual poet, emotional
       ③ Darkness to light
                Adam = sin → "upright Adam"
                Eden = garden where apples were eaten →
                                                       positive increase of faith
                Flood = terror → refuge in the Ark
       ① First Period personal problem — language limited / vocab small / repetition /
                                obsession with few words "fork "vein" "suck"
                                "worm" "deaths & entrances"
                         — sentence short / short breathed / irregular
                           in beat & length
                           eg "If my head ...
       ⑤ Second Period: charged with powerful & poignant feelings for others — luckier
                         in vocab, words disorganised, longer grammatical
                         units, eg / sentence of 3 stanzas in "Refusal ..."
                         symbols diminish → metaphors & images
       ⑥ Third Period - Faith and love — verbose, very long sentence / Adj on Adj /
                                eloquence strong / one thought even then
                                for a able poem / very hard !
       Ⓐ Dialogue "If my head ... — removes hypothetical quality / more vivid
                    (pseudo drama - several distinct people)
       Ⓑ Circumstantial ambiguity — leaves us wondering who, what, where
                                    when are
                                    — not helped by title. Only B not lives prosperous
       Ⓒ Orderly & Ongoing — makes look closely
                             — entertains emotion by regulating amount of knowledge
                             — suspense
                             — strong - plenty of meaning "bum. city 'sodomy'
                                                        full of sin - sodomy
                             — fullness "bowandarrow birds" - we often look

- wholeness
  bardic quality welsh love of music
  surrealism - wayward-ness (not a secret / not a surrealist)
              - not 'angry young man' "But today the struggle
              The concious acceptance of guilt is
                                                    necessary ...   work
GENERAL - "private social poet"
          Wee Christ all die achieve immortality for "After the first
                                                        AUDEN" ...

13.4 Effective revision

The essentials of effective revision are:

1. *Making and learning revision notes.* One student who got a First in English at Oxford had six weeks to revise six papers. He revised a paper each week. Each day he did a revision note, condensing one whole unit of work on to one side; and each day, he learned that day's revision note, *and also* went over *all* the revision notes he had made up to that point, reading and recalling. You can imagine how well he knew his work at the end of all this.

2. *Planned revision.* Students find it very hard to plan a revision programme. If you find it hard, you are not alone: underneath, you know it's essential, but somehow you don't do it. Ask your teachers to provide a plan. They've all been through what you're going through. The student above had a simple plan that worked. You need the same.

3. *Concentration.* Have you ever got to the day before an exam and said to yourself: If only I had one more day, I could do so much. You've probably had the experience of effectively revising really enormous amounts of material within days of an exam. You've probably amazed yourself. Just think how good it would be to use that level of concentration earlier.

4. *Soggy areas.* Go over well in advance any areas of the syllabus that you can't understand – or just can't stand. Read up and see your teacher. If it's still a problem, leave it out if you can; if not, try again. Some topics which seem awful are actually quite easy when you come to understand them. You may be pleasantly surprised.

5. *Past questions.* These are the best revision aid you can have. You will need practice at answering past questions under timed conditions; this is where 'crammers' are so effective – they test you out of existence! But it works. What is less well understood is that, over and above this, you need experience in analysing a wide range of questions without writing the answers out in full. Writing a few answers in full is not enough. Also use examiners' reports.

6. *Maths and languages.* Apart from revision notes, practice is vital. You will probably underestimate the amount of practice required. You actually need *'over-practice'*. Remember that your techniques have to hold up on unfamiliar material under the pressure of the exam room. Work through both previously completed questions and new questions.

Chapter 14

A Level Examinations

When the examination itself arrives, your careful preparation along the lines discussed will give you a firm basis of confidence. However, there are certain points to remember so that you ensure all your hard work gains its reward.

14.1 Relevance

More people under-achieve or fail by *not answering the question* than for any other single reason.

1. Irrelevance can arise from *misunderstanding* the question, and where this happens marks are given only for what happens to be relevant by chance.
2. The question can also be *disregarded* (in spite of having been understood at the outset) by the examinee ignoring it or by making a token gesture towards it at the beginning or the end. In such situations some observations can have relevance, and be worth a few marks.
3. *Partial* irrelevance is also common, by examinees beginning on the question and then wandering off it, or by beginning in a confused way and then working towards the question as the essay progresses. That which is relevant is credited: that which is not, is not.
4. Another error is to *twist* the question to fit a prepared line of thought. This receives a mark according to what is relevant and what is not, and the mark will be considerably lower than what could have been achieved by answering the question as set.

See diagram on p 131.

Examples of irrelevance in answer to two essay titles on an A Level General Studies paper

- What are the advantages and disadvantages of Sixth Form Colleges? Many candidates wrote about sixth form education in general.
- Do you feel yourself to be a European? Many candidates wrote on the history of the European Community.

In every examination, you must answer the question, the whole question, dealing with the issues it raises, but not going beyond that.

14.2 Tackling the paper

In tackling the paper, there are four key points to remember:

1. *Choose the questions very carefully.* This is a crucial and much neglected art: you can ruin your whole A Level by choosing the wrong questions. Take your time and weigh your choice very carefully, making sure you follow the instructions on the paper. Often, after an exam, the teacher thinks students will have chosen, say, questions 1, 3 and 5; then he finds they have chosen 2, 4 and 6 – in view of their studies, he is amazed! This is an indication of how common it is for the wrong questions to be chosen.
2. *Tackle the easiest question first.* This will not always be the compulsory question. In this way you write yourself in and give yourself confidence. You are also thinking unconsciously about the harder questions as you write. Move up the order of difficulty.
3. *Divide your time carefully between the questions.* This, like the other two points, is not spectacular knowledge, but like anything else in life, success comes to those who do the basics well. You will see from the table on p 132 that an average of 10 on each of four essays gives an E grade, whereas an average of 16 on each of four essays gives a B grade. This table is worth studying carefully.
4. *Check over your paper at the end.* Make sure you are saying what you intended to say. Weed out any errors. Any crossing out should be with a single horizontal line. Evaluation of your work is an important part of the creative process.

Ways of being irrelevant

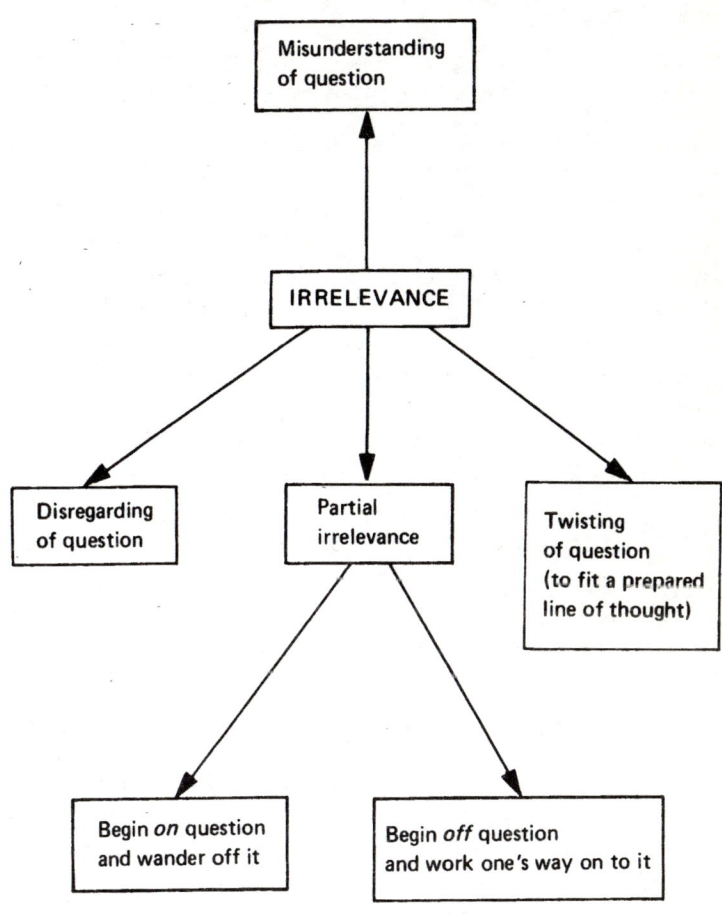

Table showing marks related to A Level grades, indicating the importance of dividing time carefully between questions

Percentage marks	A Level grade
70 and above	A
61–69	B
54–60	C
47–53	D
40–46	E
33–39	N
32 and below	U

Note 1:   4 answers at: 16 each give 64 per cent, a grade B
                        14 each give 56 per cent, a grade C
                        12 each give 48 per cent, a grade D
                        10 each give 40 per cent, a grade E

Note 2:   Each answer out of 25.

Note 3:   Grade boundaries differ subject by subject and year by year, but the above is a guide.

14.3 Writing essays in the exam room

The fundamentals which were discussed earlier still hold good, but there are slight modifications, given that this is an examination. Writing an essay in an exam is a three-stage process:

1. *React to the question.* The topics will be those with which you are familiar, but expect the questions to seem unfamiliar at first sight. The questions will make you think in some unpredictable ways – which is their intention. Look at the key words in the question and they will trigger ideas, which you then list in rough. More ideas can be generated by asking yourself questions about the question: your answers to yourself will become rough notes. Beware in particular the exact meaning of the following words:

   - *Analyse.* Break down complex issues, ideas and processes into component parts and recognise how the various parts are related.
   - *Compare.* Point out similarities or likenesses between things. In practice, this may also involve pointing out the contrasts or differences.
   - *Discuss.* Explain clearly several sides of a topic.

- *Evaluate.* Give a judgement or opinion as to the worth of something. Judgements should be reasoned and supported by arguments or facts. This is not the same as *describe*.

  Stage 1, then, involves listing ideas as they come to you by free association. Always jot down ideas the moment they come into your head. Evidence (eg, examples and quotations) is particularly important.

2. *Structure your reactions.* The next stage is to structure your reactions by forming paragraphs. This is often not done, and ideas are simply put down in their free association format. However, diffuse and rambling answers can never score high marks, even when the material is good; conversely, a structured answer tends to gain marks even when its content is comparatively thin. The desired structure of an exam essay is shown in the diagram below.

The structure of an exam essay

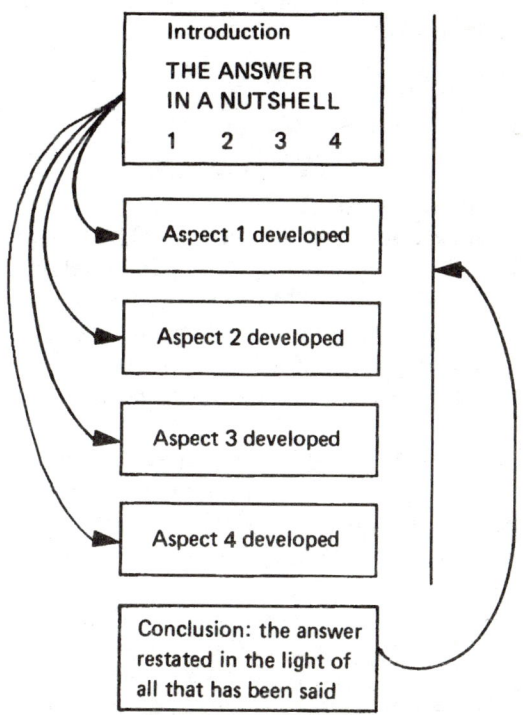

133

The answer is given in nutshell form in the first paragraph, and the major aspects of the answer are touched upon in a generalised way. This helps to ensure relevance, and it also informs the examiner of your line (a great help). Each aspect will have a paragraph to itself, and you will usually have between four and six aspects.

In answering a question, you should assume knowledge on the examiner's part: you make allusion to material as far as the answer demands, and you develop the points that you make; but it is unnecessary, counter-productive and wasteful of time to expand beyond that. The final paragraph restates the answer. This is not a simple repetition: you restate the answer in the light of all that has been said. You thereby leave your answer clearly in the examiner's mind, just before he puts a mark on it.

3. *Use good written English*. Written English is more formal than spoken English. You will probably have had a certain amount of 'discussion teaching', but you should write in formal English. Leave two lines blank between each paragraph: it makes your work easier to read.

14.4 The examiner's task

The examiner's task is almost as pressurised as your task when you write your exams. In A Level Government and Politics, for instance, each examiner could have 250–300 papers to mark in three weeks. His average is about 12–15 papers a day. Your paper gets about 15–20 minutes. In Modern Languages at A Level, the rate is about five scripts an hour, or 12 minutes each. The examiner will more often than not have his job to do during the day, so marking is done early in the morning, in the evenings and at weekends.

It is therefore clear that all the ways in which you can help the examiner will tend to dispose him favourably towards your paper. So number the questions in the same way as on the question paper; organise your work sensibly; assemble your answer sheets in the right order. Make life as easy as possible for the examiner.

Chapter 15
GNVQ Tests

The main emphasis in a GNVQ is on the portfolio, but there are also some external tests. They are on the mandatory units, not on the optional units or on the core skills units.

15.1 The nature of GNVQ tests

The tests are fixed-response tests, ie multiple choice. They last one hour, and you will have to make between 30 and 40 responses. They are sent away to be marked by machine. There are sessions three times a year and any test can be retaken.

The pass mark is 70 per cent, but don't be frightened by this. The external tests are simply to confirm that you know the underlying principles and knowledge of a particular unit and that you have breadth of coverage. As such, they are not to be feared. Having studied the unit, all you really need is common sense, familiarity with what is required, and some practice.

15.2 How to succeed in GNVQ tests

You need to see some sample papers, and to know the contents of examiners' reports. These reports are sent to centres, and it is essential that you know what's in them. You will soon acquire a comforting familiarity with what you have to do.

1. *Be fully familiar with the mechanics of the exam*:

    (a) You must use a soft HB pencil, as ink and biro cannot be machine read. Take pencils in with you.
    (b) If you want to change an answer, rub out the original lightly and make your new response. Take a rubber.

(c) You may need a calculator. Take one with you, with all the memory erased.

(d) Do any rough work on the question paper, not on the answer sheet.

(e) You will have to mark A, B, C or D on the answer sheet, and there is no set number of times each letter has to come up. Be careful that the space you are marking corresponds with the question you are answering.

(f) Only one answer is the right answer and you get one mark for each correct response you make. Marks are not deducted for incorrect responses.

2. *Have in your mind a generalised procedure for tackling the questions.* You will adapt this according to common sense and according to circumstances, but it is helpful to 'pre-set' your thinking with a sound, step-by-step procedure:

Step 1: Read the question very carefully. The precise words used will enable you to distinguish between possible answers. Work out a provisional answer before proceeding.

Step 2: Look at all the answers: sometimes a seemingly right answer (a distractor) is put in early in the list, with the correct answer coming later.

Step 3: Eliminate the answers that are wrong. This should leave you with about two possibles.

Step 4: Discriminate between the two. Both may have some truth in them but one will be closer than the other.

Step 5: Don't get stuck on a question and spend too long on it. Move on and come back to it later (making sure as always that the spaces you mark correspond with the question you are answering). At the end, make an attempt at the questions you have left out. These attempts are often right: you are well warmed up. If they're wrong, you aren't penalised.

Step 6: When you've finished, check over your answers. People can be reluctant to do this, especially with multiple choice, but corrections made at the end are often good ones, again because you are well warmed up.

15.3 GNVQ test question types

You need to be familiar with the types of test question used. They are:

1. Standard multiple choice questions

You pick A, B, C or D, only one of which is correct. Here is one example from an Advanced GNVQ in Health and Social Care (unit on Psychological and Social Aspects).

Example
Mr Cook retired to bed after lunch complaining of a pain in his upper left arm and chest. At 4 pm his wife discovered him dead.

What is the most immediate coping mechanism which Mrs Cook is likely to adopt following her husband's sudden death?

    A   acceptance
    B   depression
    C   anger
    D   denial

Comments
The key words in the question are 'most immediate' and 'sudden'. A is obviously wrong: she won't just say 'Oh well, that's that'. You might be tempted towards B, but be careful, depression is not an immediate reaction. B is a distractor. You are left with anger or denial. People can become angry as part of mourning, but tucked away at the end is the right answer, D (she cannot believe it, it can't be true). You can work this out without remembering in detail the work of Parkes and others, which has established the stages of mourning as: Denial, Anger, Depression, Acceptance.

2. Grouped multiple choice questions

Four answer options A, B, C or D are given first, followed by three questions. You choose from the four answer options A, B, C, or D, the correct answer for each of the three questions. Each answer option may be used more than once. Each of the three questions carries one mark. These are easier to do than to describe. Here is one example from an Advanced GNVQ in Leisure and Tourism.

Example
Questions 25–27 share answer options A to D.

In order to be effective, a team will normally need to be balanced, with members adopting different roles. These roles could include:

    A   team leader
    B   evaluator
    C   innovator
    D   completer

Decide which role will be taken by the team member who:

    25   Monitors the progress of the team
    26   Co-ordinates and directs the team process
    27   Contributes creative ideas

Comments
This question is testing your knowledge of Belbin's work on team roles. You know the answer to 25 (monitor) is A (evaluator), because Belbin uses the phrase 'Monitor Evaluator'. Even if you did not remember your Belbin precisely, one word would trigger the other. By common sense, 26 could only be A (Belbin's Chairman, who takes the co-ordinating role). Each answer option has to be considered each time, because each can be used more than once, but 27 is fairly obviously C (Belbin's Plant, or Innovator, who has the creative ideas).

3. Paired True–False Questions

A phrase introduces a pair of statements. Each statement is true or false. You get one mark for correctly judging both statements. Here is an example from an Advanced GNVQ in Business.

Example
Decide whether each of these statements is True (T) or False (F):

(i)   insecure computer networks can aid the spread of computer viruses
(ii) it is impossible to protect computer networks from viruses

Which option best describes the two statements?

A	(i) T	(ii) T
B	(i) T	(ii) F
C	(i) F	(ii) T
D	(i) F	(ii) F

Comments

The key words here are 'insecure' and 'can'. (i) is clearly True (T); lack of security anywhere can cause problems. In (ii), 'impossible' is a key word; always be suspicious of anything that looks like exaggeration. The other key word is 'protect'. This does not mean that protection has to be complete. By common sense, some protection is clearly possible. (ii) is False (F). B is therefore the correct answer. In True–False items, you tend to decide on the answer before looking at the options.

With practice, you will find that your confidence grows. You are likely to end up finding these questions quite enjoyable.

Chapter 16

Aiming for the Future

After spending two years on your Advanced GNVQ or on A Levels, you need to be sure that your next step is the right one.

16.1 What after your course (a gap year?)

As early as the spring of your first year of study, you need to be thinking fairly precisely about this. Clarify in your own mind the deadlines for submitting forms. Mostly this will be during the first half of the autumn term of your second year.

There are two main options: either a course or employment. Decide what to do by listing the realistic alternatives, and evaluate them. This will almost certainly involve discussions with an adviser in your college or school, or from the local careers service. Look again at decision-making on p 30. As an initial stimulus, a flow chart summary of possibilities is given on p 143.

Consider taking a gap year. Universities believe that such a year can, if productively used, provide valuable experience helping you both to contribute to, and gain from, your course. Mathematics departments, though, often prefer to take students without the gap. Around 15 per cent of students from the maintained sector, and up to 35 per cent from the independent sector, take a gap year. These are rough figures, but gap year students are certainly a minority, so don't feel you have to. If you choose to, there are two ways to set something up:

1. *Make all the arrangements yourself.* You can, for instance, look in *The Lady* for au pair work abroad, or you can write to: Peridot Press, 2 Blenheim Crescent, London W11 1NN for their publication, *The Gap Year Guidebook*, which gives you all the good leads for all the types of thing you can do, both here and abroad.

2.   *Use one of the two key organisations which help to place you*:

The Project Trust
The Hebridean Centre
Ballyhough
Argyll
PA78 6TE   Tel: 0187 93 444

GAP Activity Projects
44 Queen's Road
Reading
RG1 4BB   Tel: 01734 594914

It is a good idea to write early to these organisations, say in the summer term of your first year. For the Project Trust, you need to be between 17¼ and 19½ years old inclusive at the time of going overseas; registration closes at the end of January for those going overseas in September of that year, but early application is strongly advised. For the GAP scheme you should be 18 or 19 by the time you start your project; and you should apply by not later than April to begin the following autumn, or to begin in the New Year (you can go for between four and nine months).

16.2 Getting into Oxford or Cambridge

Oxford and Cambridge have the reputation to attract the best students. Competition is keen. At Oxford each year, 7,000 applicants apply for 3,000 places; and these applicants tend to have been pre-selected by schools or colleges. Conditional offers are most commonly AAB or ABB: 80 per cent of a year's intake at Oxford achieves ABB or better.

The college system is a particular feature of both universities. A tutorial is traditionally you, your tutorial partner and a college tutor: you need to be suitable for this style of education, though there are of course lectures as well. You also need to be sure that you like the (more traditional) courses offered. As they are only eight weeks' long, terms are intense.

However, both universities want to attract as many realistic applicants as possible, and will consider your ability against your educational and social circumstances. Potential is crucial. You need to feel there is some special reason why you should apply, more than just being talented or competent. That means, as a rule of thumb, at least five grade As at GCSE, plus ideally some A* grades.

Preparation is best done by widening your A Level work, once your A Levels are smoothly under way. This will be from the spring term onwards of your first year of A Levels. In general, do the widening out according to interest.

Attend summer term open days. Especially look out for departmental or faculty events, or college open days which are targeted at your subject: from these you can pick up valuable insight, tips and hints.

Offers are made conditional on your A Level results, but some form of enhancement can be required. Cambridge uses S Level papers or STEP papers, which are taken along with your A Levels, usually in one subject. However, except for Maths, Medicine and Veterinary Medicine, an extra examination is not necessarily required. For Oxford, you may be asked to submit written work or to take a short test before being interviewed. Both universities will also consider you after your A Levels, but for admission in the following year.

Offers are a 'sensed' or 'felt' business. You can help yourself at interview by being likeable and – most crucially – by 'thinking on your feet': a few shrewd words could be critical in getting a place.

In choosing which college, consider age (old or new), size (big or small), location (in the city, or outside) and sex (only three Oxbridge colleges are women only, the rest are mixed, so what is the real sex balance?). The big, old, inner city colleges are harder to get into.

Consult closely with your school or college.

16.3 Choosing university courses and other training

In general this takes place in the *summer term of the first year* of your A Levels or Advanced GNVQ. The autumn term of your second year is too late for this, and in any case there is too much work pressure from your ordinary study.

Choose your degree or vocational course primarily on the basis of *liking,* then look at location. Go first for the course you find most attractive. People drop out because they do not like their course: they lose motivation. Conversely, liking your course means interest, and interest means willing work. The amount of work you do in higher education is more important than being bright. Consider,

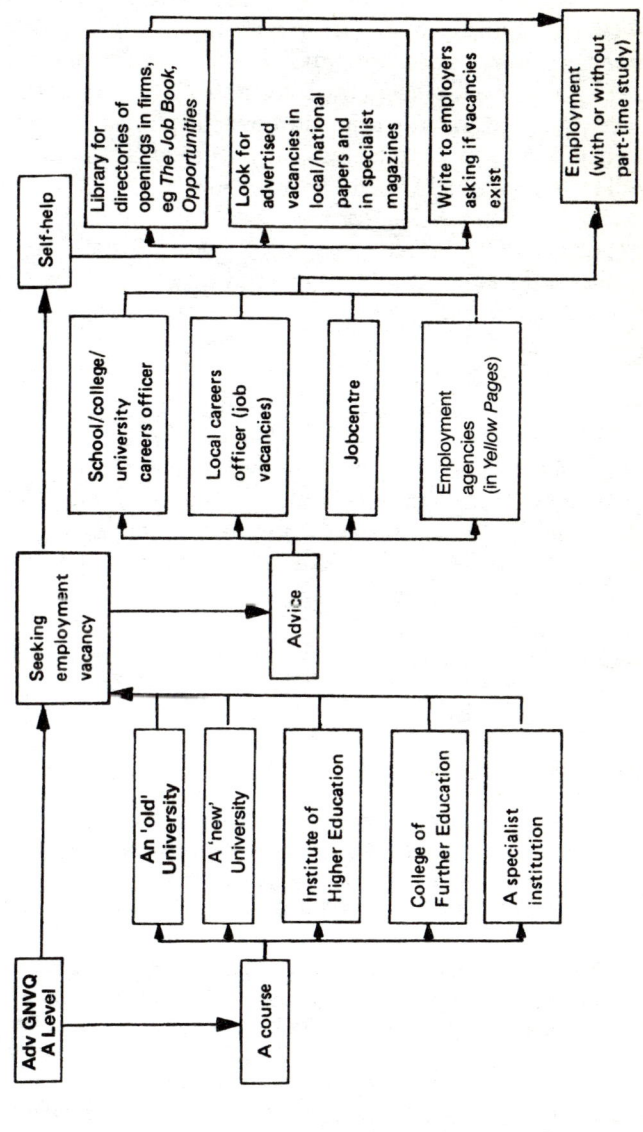

Some main employment and course routes after Advanced GNVQ or A Levels

Adv GNVQ A Level → **A course**

A course →
- An 'old' University
- A 'new' University
- Institute of Higher Education
- College of Further Education
- A specialist institution

→ **Seeking employment vacancy** → **Advice**

Advice →
- School/college/university careers officer
- Local careers officer (job vacancies)
- Jobcentre
- Employment agencies (in *Yellow Pages*)

Seeking employment vacancy → **Self-help**

Self-help →
- Library for directories of openings in firms, eg *The Job Book, Opportunities*
- Look for advertised vacancies in local/national papers and in specialist magazines
- Write to employers asking if vacancies exist

→ **Employment (with or without part-time study)**

also, how much tuition you will receive: this varies from university to university. Note, too, the balance between continuous assessment and the final exam, as this too, varies.

Now consider *location*. Is the university civic (in a town), red-brick (just outside a town) or campus (in the country)? How much accommodation is on and off site? Careful consideration of these points can make all the difference to your happiness.

Be prepared to *write* to institutions, or phone, to find out further information. Universities do not mind this, and often you will be able to obtain useful information.

Visit universities. The summer is an excellent time for this.

Ask your teachers what grades they think you'll get. Then you can apply for the courses and universities which are at the right level for you. It's no use going for Bristol, Exeter, Durham and so on if you are not likely to achieve the grades they expect. Consult *The Complete Degree Course Offers* by Brian Heap, published by Trotman, for details of likely grades and for other tips.

To find out what each university is *really like*, consult *The Times Good University Guide*, published by Times Books.

It is very important, especially if you are taking a GNVQ, to *check* whether what you are studying is suitable for the courses for which you are applying. Look again at section 1.6 on p 19, and also consult university propectuses.

A selection of career openings after degrees in the stated subjects

Subject	Career openings include:
Biology	Medical laboratory scientific officer, research, hospital biochemist, teaching, sales, management trainee
Chemistry	Research, product development, quality control, research and development, technical advisory work, teaching
Computer Science	Computer programming, software engineer, software development, systems programmer
Economics	Chartered accountant, financial management, actuary, insurance broking, investment analyst, stockbroking, management trainee
English	Teaching, secretarial, solicitor, journalism, management trainee, police, social work, chartered accountancy, librarianship, publishing

Geography	Teaching, retail management, transport planning, chartered accountancy, librarianship
History	Teaching, chartered accountancy, insurance, solicitor, retail management, advertisement sales, estate agent, management trainee
Languages	Teaching, marketing, administration, secretarial
Maths	Teaching, computer programming, software engineer, systems analyst, statistician, systems engineer, chartered accountant, actuary
Music	Teaching, advanced performing, singer, musical director, stage management
Philosophy	Higher degree, solicitor, social work, management, chartered accountant, teaching
Physics	Higher degree, research, research and development (R & D), development engineer, engineer, medical physicist, technical advisory work, electronics engineer, quality control, teaching, computer programming, systems engineer, systems analyst
Politics	Chartered accountant, financial management, insurance broking, residential social work, social work, child care work, community worker, civil service, housing management, teaching, management trainee, journalism
Psychology	Higher degree, residential social work, social work, child care work, nursing, clinical psychologist, marketing
Sociology	Residential social work, social work, voluntary work, child care work, community work, teaching, retail management, nursing, housing management, police

The changing occupational balance

Expanding occupations	Contracting occupations
Production industries	Production industries
Engineers, scientists and technologists	Support services (eg, clerical) and personal services
Technicians	Operatives
Multiple-skilled craftsmen	Single-skilled craftsmen

Service industries	Service industries
All professions	Managers, administrators, technicians, craftsmen and operatives
Support services (part time)	Support services (full time)
Personal services (part time)	Personal services (full time)

16.4 Course choice by computer

There are two good ways of gaining computerised help with your course choice.

1. Use ECCTIS

ECCTIS is a computerised database of courses at UK universities and colleges. You can use it in local careers offices, and many colleges and schools also have it. Someone will be there to help you. It is a big help in coming to the right decision. Here is an example to give you an idea of how it works.

Example of using ECCTIS

You want a first degree course in Hotel Management, with no other subject. You want it full time, in London. The computer tells you there are four such courses. One is at South Bank University. You can see that they accept GNVQs, and what A Level grades they want, along with which A Levels are especially welcome. The course is described, and there are basic statistics on the institution.

ECCTIS is very useful for finding combined degree courses, and if you have found your ideal course, enter its UCAS number, and ECCTIS will show you all the other courses like it.

The Potter section of ECCTIS tells you more about what it's like at each university. It tells you, for example, that if you want a rural university in the East Midlands, there is only Loughborough. Full details are given of campus life including accommodation.

2. Use Course Finder

You have to pay for this (about £10). You fill in a multiple choice form which asks you lots of questions about your intellectual interests, the type of institution you want and where. You also give details of the qualifications you have, and the grades you hope to get for your Advanced GNVQ or A Levels. You get back your own personal A4 booklet, giving specific details of courses which should suit you. Course Finder is especially useful if you want to go to university, but aren't yet sure what to study there. Write to: The Morrisby Organisation, 83 High Street, Hemel Hempstead, Herts HP1 3AH.

16.5 Planning a fall-back

For entry to higher education you use the Universities and Colleges Admissions Service (UCAS). This scheme applies to all full-time first degree, HND and DipHE courses except such courses in Art and Design. (If you want to go into Art, it is in any case best to do a Foundation Course first, for which you apply direct to your local college.) First degrees in Teacher training and in Nursing are within UCAS; so are those in Physiotherapy (now the only way of qualifying). However, outside the UCAS scheme are professional training courses in Nursing and Social Work.

You can choose six courses on your UCAS form. Unless you are applying for less popular courses in less popular places, consider building easier fall-backs into your choices, to cover yourself if your grades dip. For example, if you are applying for a highly competitive course such as medicine, consider having as fall-backs two choices in a *related* field such as medical sciences. Medical schools won't mind. *University and College Entrance: the Official Guide* tells you where you may get lower offers, whatever your course (see p 20); so does Heap's book (see p 144); the latter is easier to use.

The Times Good University Guide (see p 144) tells you whether a university is an old polytechnic. Such universities may offer lower grades, especially if they are in inner London, the north, or the east, rather than in the south and the west. They tend to be on split sites within cities, and to be vocationally orientated; they have more part-time students and more mature students.

Accommodation can be more difficult. But their lecturers have traditionally had fewer postgraduate students and fewer research projects, thus more time for teaching, and there is evidence that students have achieved better degree results in them than students of a similar ability have in longer-established universities.

Consider, too, the colleges and institutes of higher education. There are 51 in England and Wales. They are smaller than universities, but have a wide range of courses leading to degrees and HNDs. Some specialise; others are more diverse. About six out of ten students who follow higher education courses do so in former polytechnics and in colleges and institutes of higher education.

Don't ignore HNDs (Higher National Diplomas). They are virtually degree level, and you can in fact transfer from them to degree courses if you do well. They require a minimum one pass at A Level plus four at GCSE, ie five different subjects in all. A second subject should normally have been studied to A Level, though not necessarily passed. One Advanced GNVQ would stand in place of these A Levels.

During the summer at the end of your first year you can do some useful work in planning a fall-back. Buy the *Sunday Times*, *Sunday Telegraph* or *Observer* for all the Sundays in August. You'll see advertisements there from new universities and institutes of higher education, which will be filling up their places. Note some of the courses advertised: you can apply for them during the autumn term of your second year as a saver. During the second part of August, *The Independent* carries specific university and institute of higher education vacancies by course and institution, so pinpointing where applications might be specially welcome when you apply.

16.6 Completing a good application form

The *key* is to show motivation. This is shown by a uniform choice of degree subject (or an explanation of non-uniform choice); by good GCSE results (or weak GCSE results explained); and by a personal section which shows that you have had relevant experience, and that you are an interesting person, with several hobbies, whose distinctive personality comes through in what you've written.

The *personal section* poses the most problems, because it is simply a blank space to fill in. There is no prescribed way of doing this, but you'll find the following four suggested headings give you a good result:

- *Choice of course.* Say what you hope to get out the course, your motivation, your relevant experience and work experience. Put down evidence showing why you are right for the course.
- *Aspirations.* If you're having a gap year, give details. Put down your career aspirations.
- *Main interests.* The ones relevant to your course come first. Intellectual interests are important, but include social and sporting ones too.
- *Other activities.* Minor ones.

Then mention your motivation again at the end. You as a person must come through. Refer to music, dance and drama qualifications. Be specific about your interests, eg if you put down reading, say what. Use action words and positive words. Tell your referee any points you want him to make about you, but these should not have been included in your personal section (at UCAS, your form is 'moved around' and becomes a one-sided reduction on which your personal section is opposite the referee's report).

Abide by some *simple mechanics.* You must, by photocopying the original, perfect a rough one first, then copy it out. Watch spelling and grammar (eg, words like experience, achieve, insensitive). Write entirely in block capitals (because the form is reduced to two thirds before being sent to universities). Make sure that what you write is properly aligned. Send off the form by half term of the autumn term: technically, an early application should not give you an advantage, but in practice it may do so in competitive subjects.

If you are taking a *GNVO*, ask your higher education adviser for the model sent out by UCAS on how to put down all the parts of it; alternatively there is one in *How to Complete Your UCAS Form*, by Higgins and Lamley, published by Trotman.

16.7 Doing well in an interview

This section is specifically about university interviews. Let's look at what's really important, then illustrate that with reference to a couple of examples. The examples are written in terse, abbreviated form, so that you can pick up the flavour of what happened. These interviews were more testing than most people experience.

1. *What is really important*? The key is to think on your feet. You must provide evidence as to why you think what you think. Thinking on your feet is absolutely crucial. You might be asked to expand on something, or to re-examine something you've said. The aim is not to try to defeat you. It is to see how your mind works, and to see if you can develop and refine your thoughts. You are likely to be asked a question that you cannot answer, to see how you react when being led through the learning process. You must keep thinking and keep talking.

2. *Two interviews examined*:
    (a) *Medicine, Cambridge*. First interview in front of three medics. Something about his school, to break the ice. Then: You like Pure Maths, how does this help with Medicine? Here is a Pure Maths question to do. You enjoy genetics. How is this relevant to medicine? Then his work experience was discussed. Then: Have you any questions? He asked some points about the course. Second interview with the Admissions Tutor. Are you getting special teaching for Cambridge? Why have you applied to this College? Tell me about your gap year plans.
    (b) *English, Oxford*. First interview with one tutor. Kept asking why all the time. You have also applied to Kent for Film Studies – is film superior to literature? How are they different? What do you read besides your A Level books? You say you read *The Times* and *The Independent* – why not *The Telegraph*? Do you want to ask me anything? Second interview with one tutor. The tutor read a poem, then said: What do you think of it? Third interview with one tutor, who said: Let's talk about death in literature.

The message is clear. You have to be interested in, and enthusiastic about, what you apply for. You will therefore have thought about your subject in advance, and you will be able to think on your feet in an interview.

16.8 When the results come out

This section explains the normal course of events, though there may be minor variations from year to year. The days mentioned refer to A Levels, but GNVQ students will also need to know how to proceed with their UCAS applications.

If you have been a *boarder* at a college or school, make sure well in advance that UCAS has a new forwarding address to replace your college address for correspondence. This should be a UK address, and someone should be there to cover the post, preferably you!

Issue of results

Results arrive in college or school on the morning of a Thursday in the middle of August. They are then sent to you, or you can probably collect them. Universities get your results direct from the Boards on the previous Monday, so they can start work on them.

1. *If you've made your grades for your firm or insurance offers*: Celebrations can begin! Confirmation literature will be sent to you from UCAS between the Friday of results week and the following Friday. Do what it says. If you will be getting a grant, tell your local education authority your results and where you're going. Make sure you have a bank account to receive your maintenance grant.

2. *If you've just missed your grades for your firm or insurance offers*: Ring the university and make your case! It comes best from you (it isn't really best if it's your college, and it shouldn't be your parents). A letter from you to the university is also a good idea, as this is put on your file and seen when your case is reviewed. (However, do not make contact with a university *if* you have specifically been asked by them not to.) Universities decide marginal cases at the beginning of the week after results Thursday, so they may not be able to give you an answer when you ring. You may be made a changed course offer or a changed year offer. UCAS, too, will be in touch with you.

3. *If you are well wide of your grades for both your firm and insurance offers*: you must talk with an adviser.

   Clearing vacancies are published in *The Independent* on the

Wednesday after the previous results Thursday, and on following days; from that Wednesday onwards, you will also be able to get on-line vacancy data through ECCTIS in your college, or at the local careers office. The newspapers will be full of vacancy advertisements, and some advertisements will appear *before* results Thursday both in the press (particularly the Sunday press), and also on Teletext on Channel 4, pp. 644–648.

But you can ring around for a place *before* the Wednesday on which official vacancies are known; early action is vital. Hit the phone. Have your UCAS number ready. Ask for Admissions. If there's a course that seems suitable for you, you may be transferred to an Admissions Tutor. Be ready to justify yourself. He or she can then ask you for your clearing form. If you have been turned down by your firm and insurance choices, you'll get clearing documentation automatically from UCAS, usually around the Wednesday or Thursday of the week following results Thursday. You can send your clearing form to only one university at a time. Be ready to make some 40 or 50 calls if necesary. Expect the ringing round to last for several days, though it may in fact be over quite quickly. Be prepared to consider alternative courses. Whatever your situation, there's something that can be done. Ring your adviser or go in and see him.

Appealing against your results

You may feel like appealing against your results. This must be done through your school or college, who must feel there is a serious discrepancy between your actual, and expected, results. Rarely are results changed, and then only after delay. Using irrelevant material in exam answers is the most common explanation for a result lower than expected. Remember it is common practice for schools to send in expected grades. Boards check these against actual grades, and check discrepancies; all this will have already been done when you receive your results. If you press ahead with an appeal, take other initiatives in addition.

Retaking

You may consider re-taking your A Levels, if you feel you can do better and view the prospect positively. The options are:

1. return to school or college, though this may feel like taking a step backwards;
2. take a correspondence course, where you will need the motivation to work on your own;
3. go to a college of further education locally – their provisions vary;
4. go to a 'crammer'. They are effective but expensive, and tend to be concentrated in London and Oxford. Free information about them can be obtained from Gabbitas Truman and Thring Educational Trust, 6–8 Sackville Street, Piccadilly, London W1X 2BR.

16.9 Into employment

You may decide to go into work directly after your Advanced GNVQ or A Levels, but even if you don't start work then, you will obviously go into employment eventually. Your local careers service is there to help you, and if you are a graduate, you have your university's careers service, or that of a nearby university.

The following may surprise you. It will help you to find the job that you want:

15 per cent of jobs are gained through replying to adverts in:

local newspapers
national newspapers
trade magazines
shop windows
specialist papers
local library

10 per cent of jobs are gained through agencies:

employment agencies
head hunters
Jobcentres
job clubs (ask at Jobcentre)

75 per cent of jobs are gained through the direct approach:

personal contacts
networking
past employer

    nepotism
    the pub
    friends
    family
    phoning
    mail shot

The message is clear: *go for the direct approach.*

When trying a mail shot, target a specific person in advance. In the first paragraph of your letter, make your purpose clear. In the second paragraph, cite a relevant achievement. In the third paragraph, close, looking forward to hearing from them. Do not mention money. Use your business letter format as on p 67.

Persistence is essential: you need a large number of attempts over a span of time, without becoming discouraged.

Find companies by consulting:

Chamber of Trade and Commerce
Professional organisations
Thomson Directory
Trade directories
Yellow Pages
Newspapers
Libraries

The following books from Kogan Page will help you to get and keep the job that you want

On **choosing a career**:
    Barrett J and Williams G (1990). *Test Your Own Aptitude.*
    Ball B (1989). *Manage Your Own Career.*
    Burston D (1994). *The A–Z of Careers and Jobs.*

On **job hunting**:
    Greenwood D (1994). *The Job-Hunter's Handbook. An A–Z of Tried and Tested Techniques.*
    ed Hamil S (1992). *Britain's Best Employers?*

On **application forms and letters**:
    Corfield R (1992). *How You Can Get That Job.*

On **interviews**:

Parkinson M (1994). *Interviews Made Easy: How to Get the Psychological Advantage.*

Yate M J (1992). *Great Answers To Tough Interview Questions.*

On **selection tests**:

Bryon M and Modha S (1991). *How to Pass Selection Tests.*

On **starting out in your job**:

Donald V and Grose R (1993). *Your First Job.*

Index

Index